Acknowledgments

CW01502229

Like many concerned in the management of law firms, I first acquired management responsibilities by force of circumstance, and without any formal training. I had however been lucky enough to be involved with the national aspects of Lions Clubs International, and am grateful for the help of many within that splendid organisation, particularly fellow solicitor Colin Vincent, for engendering my interest in what makes organisations tick.

The first person to get me interested in the practical application of the theory of management within law firms, and the concept of quality management in particular, was Matthew Moore, who has probably done more for the advancement of professional law firm management in this country than anyone else, and I owe much to him accordingly.

I then had the privilege of undertaking the MBA course in Legal Practice Management at Nottingham Law School, and there are two groups of people involved there who helped to make that a fascinating – if exhausting! – experience. Professor Stephen Mayson, whose brainchild the course was, and his team, especially Chris Stoakes, were a major creative influence. The other group is my fellow members of 'Hemmings & Co' (a hypothetical firm which had more management problems in our two years together than any real one could expect in a lifetime!) with whom it was a pleasure to work, namely: Kate Blackburn; Isabella Freeman; James Hillard; Jean Hindmoor; and Simon Stell.

In recent years it has been very rewarding to work with all concerned with the Law Society's Law Management Section, the staff being very ably led by Maureen Miller, and the Executive by Nicola Manning and latterly Nick Jarrett-Kerr. Many of the ideas put forward in this book have resulted from discussions, seminars and conferences promoted by that Section.

As to the book itself, my thanks are due to all those who, during its creation, have allowed me to bounce ideas off them! Their help has been much appreciated, but they bear no responsibility for the views expressed in this book.

Lastly, my thanks to the book's editor, Jane Withey, for her patience with me in what has had to be a longer process than either of us would have wished; and who has managed to control my more long-winded excesses with grace and humour.

SIMON YOUNG
April 2003

Abbreviations

CLS	Community Legal Service
CPD	continuing professional development
HR	human resources
IIP	Investors in People
ISO	International Standards Organisation
IT	information technology
KM	knowledge management
LAFQAS	Legal Aid Franchise Quality Assurance Standard
LCD	Lord Chancellor's Department
Lexcel	the Law Society's Practice Management Standards
LLP	limited liability partnership
LLP Act	Limited Liability Partnerships Act 2000
LMS	Law Management Section of the Law Society
LSC	Legal Services Commission
MDP	multi-disciplinary partnership
P&L	profit and loss account
ROI/ROC	return on investment/capital
SIF	Solicitors' Indemnity Fund
WIP	work in progress

New Partner's Guide to Management

Related titles by Law Society Publishing

Profitability and Law Firm Management
Andrew Otterburn
1 85328 820 9

Setting Up and Managing a Small Practice (2nd edition)
Martin Smith
1 85328 792 X

Solicitors' Guide to Good Management (2nd edition)
Trevor Boutall and Bill Blackburn
1 85328 732 6

Quality Management for Law Firms
Matthew Moore
1 85328 715 6

Lexcel Practice Excellence Kit (2nd edition)
The Law Society
1 85328 700 8

Excellent Client Service
Heather Stewart
1 85328 777 6

Marketing, Management and Motivation
Dianne Bown-Wilson and Gail Courtney
1 85328 810 1

Becoming a Partner
Young Solicitors Group
1 85328 841 1

Marketing Your Law Firm
Lucy Adam
1 85328 745 8

Titles from Law Society Publishing can be ordered from all good legal bookshops or direct from our distributors, Marston Book Services (tel. 01235 465656 or e-mail law.society@marston.co.uk). For further information or a catalogue, call our editorial and marketing office on 020 7320 5878.

New Partner's Guide to Management

Simon Young

The Law Society

Simon Young has asserted the right under the Copyright, Designs and Patents Act 1988 to be identified as author of this work.

© Simon Young 2003

ISBN 1 85328 776 8

Published in 2003 by the Law Society
113 Chancery Lane, London WC2A 1PL

Typeset by J&L Composition, Filey, North Yorkshire
Printed by TJ International Ltd, Padstow, Cornwall

Contents

Introduction – a new partner's perspective

The aim of this book

The object of this book is to illustrate the managerial world of a law firm from the point of view of someone who is about to become, or has just become, a partner in that firm. It seeks to draw attention to the distinctions which will be found in practice as a result of the sudden and sharp shift from being an employee, with few or no managerial responsibilities, to being a part owner and manager of a complex business. It looks to what the new partner should, and reasonably can, expect from that transformation, as well as considering what the expectations of those who were his employers, but are now his peers, are likely to be.

No offence is intended to female members of the profession by references in the text to the solicitor as 'he', for which please read 'he or she' as appropriate.

The book as an introduction to management

In some ways this is a management 'starter kit'. It covers all the main areas addressed by standard management texts, but seeks to do more than simply restate their principles. Areas that will not have a particular significance to new partners, as against partners and managers generally, will not be treated in great detail, and reference will be made to other standard texts.

Using management literature

Indeed, it is hoped that readers will be sufficiently interested by the management techniques which they encounter that they will want to know more about them. At the end of the book, therefore, is a suggested further reading list. This is admittedly a subjective listing, for there are literally thousands of management books, although a relatively small proportion of them concentrate on professional service firms, and fewer still on just law firms.

Training in management techniques

In some instances, readers may feel that management books are sufficient to draw their attention to areas where they acknowledge their skills are lacking, but feel they would benefit from some more formal training on a subject, either because it is technically difficult to master (e.g. accounting) or because it involves a practical personal skill which is better conveyed in a training environment (e.g. making presentations). Again, therefore, there is at the end of the book a list of a few of the many providers of management and personal skills training.

The place of management in a law firm

Many lawyers – and, sadly, some partners – do not appreciate that they will require management skills. This book starts by examining the role of management within the business unit that is a law firm, and the commercial characteristics of that unit. It considers what constitutes success for a firm, and hence what part a new partner is likely to have to play in working towards that success, as well as what his fellow partners' expectations of him will be. It analyses briefly some of the many different roles which a partner will be called upon to play, and points out the difficulties that can arise from this suddenly imposed plurality of roles.

Options for business vehicles

The commercial landscape for law firms is changing. At the time of writing, there are a number of possible major changes on the horizon, such as the introduction of multi-disciplinary partnerships (MDPs), and the possibility of solicitors who are employed by commercial concerns providing legal services direct to the public. Some possibilities beyond the standard concept of partnership are however already with us, and so consideration is given to the various structures within which lawyers can currently operate, and what the implications are of each, especially in terms of areas such as tax treatment and potential risk and personal liability. Ways in which individuals should look to protect themselves through partnership documentation are discussed, as are the consequences of the choice of each of the various different management and capital structures.

Systematic management

The topic of systematic management is looked at in some detail. This may be more familiar to readers either as 'quality management' or 'risk management'. The concepts of attempting to structure a firm's operations around consistent working systems, to improve efficiency and reduce error, are looked at, as are the various external awards or kitemarks which encourage and recognise efforts in this field. The impact of this approach on risk control, and hence (amongst other things) professional indemnity insurance premiums, is stated.

Strategic planning

Emphasis is placed upon the necessity for strategic development and business planning for firms. A guide is offered for the new partner on what he should be looking for in the firm's existing planning arrangements, and what techniques he may wish to deploy, either to assess for himself the wisdom of the existing efforts, or to offer as ways of remedying any existing omissions. Any type of work which the firm may consider continuing, seeking or dropping will have linkages to external forces, human and technical resources, financial consequences, and risk elements. All of these are reviewed. Ways of formulating a plan, and also the methods by which it can be turned into action, are discussed.

Marketing techniques

The way in which any business turns its business plan into reality is dependent on the success or failure of its marketing planning – indeed, this is really just a sub-set of the business plan, since the latter involves the identification of the services the business wishes to offer, the groups to which those services are to be offered, and how it intends to deliver those services. Any marketing efforts are in effect the communication of those plans. The techniques by which that communication can be effected – if you like, the toolkit from which partners can choose – are set out in practical form.

Managing staff

One of the most important, and most difficult, transitions that a new partner is called upon to make is the change in status from employee to employer. Many partners will find that, immediately upon their promotion, they are asked to take on some personnel management responsibilities, even if only within a small compass. They may be responsible for hiring staff, and so recruitment and induction considerations are reviewed. They are likely to be involved in processes such as staff appraisals, and so matters relating to the setting and reviewing of goals, the planning of training, and the reviewing of the success of these efforts are all examined. Some personal issues which may arise are dealt with, as are the particular requirements of proper management of teamworking. Lastly, the particular problems posed by grievances and disciplinary matters are faced.

Accounts and finance

Two chapters of this book are concerned with financial matters. First, the finances of the firm are considered. The new partner's attention is drawn to certain key performance indicators which will help to demonstrate the state of the firm's financial health. His own investment of time and money are part of this picture. Profitability is discussed at various levels, from that of the firm down through departmental to individual level. Ways in which the firm can effectively 'benchmark' its performance, to see how it is doing in comparison with its peers, are set out.

Treatment of profits

The second financial chapter considers what rewards the new partner may expect to receive i.e. the ways in which the profits of the firm may be expected to be dealt with. The cashflow issue of drawings, replacing of course the salary the new partner has been used to, is covered. Indeed, in his early days as a partner, he may enjoy – if that is the right term! – the often encountered but conceptually odd and unattractive status of a salaried partner, and so the consequences for those in that position are considered. Many partners will be required, initially and/or by subsequent retention of profit and its conversion to capital, to build up a capital base in the firm. The possibility of a return on that capital by way of the awarding of interest is then discussed, prior to an examination of the myriad ways in which partners may decide – with important consequences – to divide their profits between themselves.

Personal development

It is trite, but nonetheless true, to refer to the legal profession as a 'people business'. An examination of this therefore starts from the perspective of the one person nearest and dearest to the heart of the new partner – himself! A great many attitudinal and developmental changes are needed upon becoming a partner, and the need for the individual to reflect on what those changes mean for him in personal terms is identified. Some of the skills needed are dealt with and, in particular, ways in which time management can be improved in order to cope with the extra burden are suggested. Skills needed for dealing with the expectations of the existing partners as to the new partner's roles as an entrepreneur and marketeer, and as a manager of people, are identified and explained. Reference is also made to the problems of management of stress, and the difficulty of dealing with the mass of information that a new partner will need to handle.

1

Management within a professional service firm

In this chapter consideration is given to the various tasks which managers within a law firm are called upon to carry out, in the light of a suggested definition of a law firm. The constituent parts which go to make up the firm are outlined, and the ways in which service delivery is converted into money are discussed. The chapter then considers what will constitute success for a new partner in the light of those factors, and examines the problems faced by new partners as a result of the multiplicity of roles that they are required to perform in order to achieve that success.

Managing the business unit

Introduction

This chapter sets out to identify and define the relationship between two aspects of a law firm: namely, its function as a provider of legal services, and its function as a business unit. It examines why that business unit requires managers. It considers what may constitute 'success' for a firm, and what driving factors underlie this success, to show the contribution played by managerial roles. A look is taken at the conflict between the roles a partner is expected to perform as fee earner on the one hand, and as manager/entrepreneur on the other, and the consequent possibility of 'role overload'.

The law firm as a business unit

The biggest single gap in understanding between a senior fee earner and a partner (a gap, it has to be said, which some will never manage to cross) is between the concept of a firm as an organisation which exists to satisfy the client-driven imperatives of turning the work round, i.e. winning the case, completing the deal etc., and the concept of the firm as a business the purpose of which is to make money. The business happens to achieve that aim by supplying those client services, but it is no different from a maker of widgets in that it is driven by the need for profit.

The historical concept

Historically, the concept of a service-oriented profession deriving its raison d'être from providing public benefit, and being a cut above those engaged in the somewhat demeaning matter of trade, was encouraged by the structure and approach of the organisations behind the 'honourable professions'. Clients were, in general, unsophisticated in their expectations, unable to gain access to jealously guarded skills and knowledge, and mostly deferential. Advertising or 'touting' was the ultimate sin, so competition played little part in professional life. In economic terms there was little need for capital intensive investment, and a scale-based charging system was set at levels which would provide a comfortable income.

The current situation

Now, however, the picture is entirely different. Clients have much higher expectations not just of professional ability but also service delivery standards and prices. Other sources of information, e.g. the internet, are vying with traditional delivery methods. Competition is a dominant factor. Information technology (IT) requirements bring with them heavy capital requirements. Price sensitivity is a reality at all levels. How then can a law firm exist as a successful business in this environment?

Defining the law firm

One comprehensive definition of a law firm is offered by Mayson:[1]

> A law firm is a business unit wholly owned by lawyers[2] comprising lawyers of varying degrees of expertise and experience, together with support staff. By co-operating with each other and with clients, these people must achieve the firm's business objectives. Those objectives are to match the legal and managerial know-how within the firm to clients' needs for legal services, and to deliver those services, in such a way that economic and other benefits result both to clients and to the law firm. Decisions about the business objectives to be followed, and the way in which they are realised, will together create and reflect the firm's mission, culture and values.

The law firm as a business unit

Note the primacy of the firm as a 'business unit', and the role of the client as a stakeholder in the money-making tasks of the firm. The new partner needs to absorb this reality. There is also much else for him to learn from this definition. He can see his place amongst the range of 'expertise and experience', and he can appreciate the equal status given to the 'legal and managerial' skills needed for attainment of the firm's proper aspirations.

He can understand the importance of the intangible factors of 'the firm's mission, culture and values', which he will be expected to adopt and develop, in setting the path to attainment of those objectives.

The people who make up the firm

The identity of a law firm can be looked at in two ways – what it is and what it does. Each helps to throw some light on the role of management. The most basic constituent part of any firm is the people who operate it, from senior partner to office junior. With the exception of one-person firms which operate with no administrative assistance, all firms will employ a range of people. The management of people, usually now referred to as human resources or HR management, is one of the most complex aspects of any business's management matrix. It involves a range of skills, from the 'soft' end of the spectrum, where personal relationships and aptitudes play a major part, to the 'hard' or technical end, where professional and legal skills need to be brought to bear.

The personal skills required of a manager will include the ability to:

- communicate effectively;
- empathise with fellow employees;
- gain the respect of fellow employees;
- give clear instructions and ensure that these are followed;
- organise working practices and patterns; and
- deal with equality and diversity issues in an appropriate manner.

Tasks which may be the responsibility of a manager will include:

- managing the recruitment and induction of new staff;
- evaluating the performance of himself and others;
- determining the training needs of those within the team;
- assessing progress in an objective manner;
- adjudicating disputes;
- taking disciplinary measures; and
- making dismissals.

Any new partner will need to accept that, as his career progresses, he will face many situations where these skills will be needed.

The business premises

Needless to say, the firm will need premises from which to operate (save to the extent to which it may choose to develop remote or 'virtual' working practices). It may well be, of course, that a new partner has little role to play initially in the selection of premises, but as the firm grows and his seniority within the firm develops, it is likely that he will at some time be involved in issues regarding the choice of premises. Beyond that, he is likely to have a part to play in arranging those aspects of the premises pertinent to him and his department, for instance: what arrangements are made for the reception of clients; the layout of the office; the choice between open-plan and traditional formats, etc. Depending on the size of firm, some tasks related to the day-to-day operation of the premises – so-called 'facilities management' – may also be allocated to him, e.g. who is responsible for arranging repairs if the lift fails, or for making sure that fire drills are carried out? Even in larger firms, newly created partners may be surprised by the readiness of employees to assume that, because the partner is now one of 'them', he has a role to play in such matters and is thus a suitable person to question or to complain to.

IT systems

It is trite to say that IT (and its attendant costs) are playing an ever-increasing part in the life of any law firm, and that the rate of change (and consequently obsolescence) is expanding exponentially, but this is nonetheless true. Any partner, even if fully supported by an IT management team, needs to keep up-to-date with what is on offer to those working in his field, and to ensure that the IT which is provided is utilised to its maximum advantage, so as to get the best return on the firm's investment. So, for example, a partner in a personal injury department should be aware of the dedicated case management systems available, what would be the advantages of using such systems, and whether his staff are both fully trained to use the installed systems, and are embracing and making the most of such usage. Only thus will he know that the work is being done at the right level of expertise, so maximising his department's profitability. He should also be looking to the future and trying to identify what changes IT may bring about. It is simply no longer acceptable for any partner to say that he is 'merely' a lawyer who does not understand IT. His task as a partner is to maximise the potential and profitability of the department for which he has or shares responsibility, and it is these days completely impossible to discharge that responsibility without a good understanding of the IT implications.

The 'knowledge capital' of the firm

The least tangible, but most important, factors which the firm's people bring to it are their knowledge and experience, whether gained before or during their time with the firm. One of the most difficult tasks for partners is to ensure that this highly ephemeral and portable knowledge is available to as many people as need it within the firm, and that it remains within the firm after the departure of those individuals who have garnered it. Mayson[3] speaks of this as 'knowledge capital' and has discussed the possibility of valuing this wholly intangible asset, just as any other capital asset within a firm is valued. The task of harvesting, storing and distributing this capital is referred to as Knowledge Management (KM). It overlaps, of course, with IT, but is by no means entirely IT dependent. Any partner will have a part to play in ensuring that the firm's KM capabilities are maximised, even if that task extends no further than ensuring that those around him (who may see no advantages, and perhaps even some disadvantages, in conferring 'their' knowledge upon others) comply with the requirements of the firm's systems in this respect. The likelihood is, however, that the partner's role will be a much more important one, requiring him to identify the KM needs of the firm/department and constantly developing and expanding the means of capturing that knowledge.

Supply of legal services by the firm

So, the firm has acquired its staff, housed them, given them the tools needed for the job, and ensured that it controls their knowledge base. What does it do with these inputs? What is its output, and what relevance has that for management issues? The simple part of the answer is of course that the firm supplies its clients with legal services. That, however, presupposes a great deal.

Selecting the services to be supplied

The first task is to identify the services to be provided. The chances are that the founder of the firm was prepared to do whatever work came his way.[4] Many firms prided themselves for years on being 'full service firms', i.e. offering the whole range of traditional legal services. Few will still make the same claim. The need for increased specialisation to keep up with technical developments and expectations, together with changes in funding arrangements and alterations in institutional clients' buying habits – all these and other factors have tended to mean that more and more firms have trimmed the range of their services. This may vary from simply cutting out certain areas (e.g. crime or publicly funded work), to concentrating on one or two niche practice areas. Equally, some firms have deliberately moved up a gear, and invested in their future by committing themselves to providing services which traditionally were seen as the bailiwick of large City firms only. Any of these choices, which can never be seen as static, involve management decisions. Any partner, however new, will be involved in at least the incremental development of the range of his department's services as dictated by day-to-day client demands and opportunities.[5]

Identifying the clients

Another area where the pace of change has been rapid is with regard to clients. No so long ago, it was a professional black mark to take a client who 'belonged' to another firm, even if the decision to move was that of the client and there was no element of solicitation. The current position could hardly be more different. Furthermore, the other side of that traditional coin, the loyalty felt by the clients themselves, has changed wholly. Few now consider themselves bound to instruct 'their' solicitor if a more attractive offer comes along (although inertia may well still play a part). Many institutional clients, which used to select their legal service providers at local level (e.g. branch offices of insurers or banks) now do so only at national level, and use their financial muscle, like supermarkets, to pressure their suppliers into lower costs or different charging structures. This may be by repeated tendering operations, reductions in panel sizes, and the threat that: 'If you won't do it our way and at our price, there are plenty of others out there who will'. A great deal of managerial time therefore needs to be spent, at all levels, on:

- retaining existing clients;
- attracting new clients;
- expanding the range of services on offer to those clients; and
- participating in the tendering process.

Delivering the services

Having identified the services to be offered, and established the client base to whom those services are to be delivered, the next step is to consider the means by which that delivery is to take place. Again, this used to be fairly straightforward. Communication was face-to-face, by letter, or by telephone, and documents were on paper. The pace at which matters were expected to move forward was dedicated by the limitations of those methods of communication. However, e-mail is now the chosen means of communication of many, and almost instantaneous replies are expected. Documents pass as e-mail attachments. The internet may be used for the communication of information either on a static basis, or an interactive one. Extranets facilitate direct client or other third party access to information held on the firm's systems. Some clients even require direct access to all data on their files. The management challenges posed by these developments are manifold. There is the task of configuring the IT systems to keep up with the requirements of clients and others, and even to move ahead of them if possible, i.e. to attract clients by innovation. There is the challenge of preserving confidentiality and security. There are the risk management elements applicable to providing communications and advice at a speed which allows little opportunity for them to be vetted.

All these areas require constantly adaptable systems within the firm at all levels, and all partners can expect to play a part in the development of those systems, and to bear responsibility for ensuring compliance with them.

Turning delivery into money

There is a lamentable tendency for many lawyers to consider that their roles end once financial matters are to be considered. They may or may not have had any part to play in providing the environment in which clients and services were selected, but they will have been instrumental in the provision of those services. The sordid consideration of the monetary consequences is the problem of the eternally present 'someone else'. Whatever the truth of that picture at less senior levels, it ceases to have any verity when it comes to partners, for it is their own money which is at stake, and their inter-partner fiduciary duties mean that each must seek to maximise the profits for the benefit of others. After all, as long ago as 1890 it was recognised that profit is an indispensable element of any partnership, when the Partnership Act defined the relationship of partnership as one which is carried on 'with a view of profit'. Accounting matters are discussed in Chapter 7, but in broad terms the role of management is to ensure that processes exist which are sufficiently robust to withstand external examination and audit for:

- billing work done;
- collecting those debts;
- managing the firm's banking arrangements;
- producing the firm's accounts;
- paying staff and other suppliers;
- managing the firm's working capital requirements; and
- paying partners their profits.

It is astonishing to discover how many partners still appear to believe that the last of those steps can occur independently of the others!

Promoting a positive culture within the firm

This might appear to be the end of the cycle. Suitable employees have been recruited, and provided with the means to do their job. The services to be offered have been recognised, the clients acquired, and the legal work performed. The work has been billed, the accounts have been controlled, the staff and other suppliers have been paid, and the partners have received their drawings. What else is there?

The answer is that, hovering somewhere above all of this, is the completely indefinable, but nonetheless vital, concept of the culture of the firm. All of these stages involve that most difficult of industrial devices, the human being, and not all of the factors which motivate people are monetary. For example, they will wish to: enjoy what they do; work in an atmosphere of mutual respect and trust; meet the intellectual challenges posed to them; to deal (as clients or as colleagues) with people they like and can relate to socially; and balance their working lives against life outside the office.[6] The culture of a firm is like the traditional description of an elephant – no-one can adequately describe it, but everyone can instantly recognise it. Nowhere does it become more recognisable than when under threat, e.g. in a merger where two cultures come into conflict. Management should recognise what characterises their particular firm's culture in order to nurture those elements of which they approve, and to move away from what they perceive as its negative aspects. It is vital that new partners immediately acknowledge and espouse this challenge. It is, for instance, a potential source of long-term problems for a new partner in a firm which prides itself on a culture of open and friendly staff relations, to become offhand when dealing with his erstwhile colleagues simply because of the elevation in his status – but it happens.

What is success for the new partner?

The change in perception upon attaining partnership

In many ways any career is defined by its aspirations, and hence the perception of what constitutes success. Prior to attaining partnership, a lawyer's concepts of success are likely to have been twofold. First, there will have been the essential technical success of providing legal services which have satisfied the clients' expectations, whether this be by winning cases, ensuring that deals are concluded or whatever. Secondly, there will have been success in the firm's internal terms, i.e. in meeting whatever targets have been set, such as billing levels, chargeable hours recorded, etc. Promotion to partnership is likely to be perceived as demonstrating that he has been successful in those respects, so that his superiors have recognised his talents and welcomed him as an equal. A trap to avoid is the temptation to view partnership as the only relevant goal, and to rest upon one's laurels. Many freshly created partners underperform in the early years of their partnership status.

The additional challenges of partnership

The reality is that all those personal markers of success will continue, so that the new partner will be expected to intensify his previously successful performance pattern. However, he will also be expected to espouse a great number of other criteria which will define whether he is a success as a partner within the firm and, flowing from that, whether the firm of which he is now part-owner and part-manager is itself successful. In other words, the range of success markers will be greatly increased, thus bringing considerable stresses in adjusting to these additional burdens.

Success factors for firms

Financial success

Every firm will (or should!) have its own business plan, and hence its own definition of what will constitute success over a given period. Ideally, these goals will have been expressed in measurable terms, so that achievement can be quantified. There are likely to be a number of common themes. One goal, which may well be publicly announced, especially to staff, is simply percentage growth in turnover. Law firms love to trumpet that they have 'grown' x per cent in the last year. This naturally produces pressures on the partners to ensure that there is a growth in client demand for work, with all that this entails in marketing terms. Another, which is not usually made public, is the amount of profit the firm is making. This may, of course, move in parallel with turnover, but only if the cost ratios remain the same. There is thus a requirement for the partner to ensure that work is done at minimum cost and maximum efficiency. This involves making sure that all employees have the systems and tools which will enable them to work at maximum efficiency (work better) and then use that efficiency to their full capacity (work harder). The partner will be expected to play his part in facilitating those circumstances, and may find that he has to make demands of employees who were, until recently, his fellow workers. The partner will of course also be subject to exactly the same demands himself when dealing with clients.

Prestige

In addition to financial goals, most firms will seek to make their mark in public terms. Often, they will try to justify this in terms of its effect on future revenues, and describe it as 'profile-raising'. Behind this, however, is the desire for recognition from the public and from the firm's peers. The new partner will be expected to play his part in this. Mostly, the inputs required will fall under the broad heading of marketing, but they may still be very varied. At one end of the spectrum will be headline-grabbing legal achievements. From there, success factors will vary from attracting high-profile new clients; the use of professional talents in such things as seminar presentations, article writing etc.; through to personal pro bono contributions to community ventures. All these will increase the pressures on the new partner's time, without necessarily producing any tangible results. Just as a firm's 'culture' was described above as indefinable but recognisable, so the factors which make a firm successful are difficult to pin down, but most firms will know whether or not they are perceived as successful.

Success as the opposite of failure

Success is usually considered in terms of positive outcomes, such as growth, profit, prestige, and profile-raising. Unfortunately, the firm's management will also have to have a very keen eye on negative factors, i.e. avoiding failure not only for its own sake but also for the huge knock-on effect it may have on performance and reputation. Most solicitors, when considering such issues, think solely of professional negligence, and indeed any new partner will have a part to play in the supervisory roles appropriate for case handling. Wise firms will, however, be thinking far beyond those narrow concepts, and looking at broader issues. How badly, for instance, could a firm's prestige and pockets be damaged by an (uninsured) sex, race, or disability discrimination claim with all its attendant publicity? What damage could be done to a professional firm's reputation by a single instance of dreadful misjudgement, such as that of Andersen in the Enron scandal, or by failing to ensure that checks and balances are in place to prevent rogue actions, such as the role of Nick Leeson in the demise of Barings? The new partner should realise that a major element of his new status is the role of policeman, keeping an eye on the actions of those around him. Sadly, the pressures of that task are intensified by the reality that in many cases the offenders he needs to guard against are his fellow partners, not the firm's staff, whether this be the result of their refusing to comply with protective systems on the basis that 'I've always done it that way', or because of fraud.[7]

Time conflicts

All of these extra pressures inevitably produce considerable difficulties in various ways. Perhaps the most easy of these to recognise is the extra time burden caused by adding a partner's duties to the existing caseload. Many partners fail to cope with this change. They either fail to carry out all that is required of them (usually by neglecting their management duties rather than their client work, since they do not recognise management as 'proper' work, and they succumb to the pressures exerted by demanding clients); or increase their working time to the extent that their personal lives, and quite possibly their health, suffer. Few actually sit down and address the time management issues which their promotion raises, or discuss these issues with their partners and colleagues, in order to try to reconfigure their working lives in a way that will allow the various tasks to be carried out. Chapter 9 deals with some ways in which this difficulty can be overcome.

Role conflicts

As outlined above, a considerable range of roles are added to a lawyer's normal tasks when he becomes a partner. Suddenly, as the part-owner of a business, he is concerned about its financial health; he must try to understand the accounts and recognise danger signals; he becomes involved in the politics which, to a greater or lesser degree, bedevil all partnerships in their decision-taking processes; he becomes responsible for the administrative tasks associated with running the business and his area of it; he becomes an employer in relation to those who were his colleagues; and he must act as a marketeer and entrepreneur in relation to the continued success and expansion of the firm. How is he to juggle these roles? The question here is not one of time management, but of self-perception. What does the new partner think of himself as being? This question is important since an individual is unlikely to be successful in a role which he does not really believe is his. Thus, if a partner does not think of himself as being, in part, a marketeer, the chances are that he will not function as such, and that important element of his overall role as a partner will be missing.

Role overload

This problem of role overload, i.e. where the difficulty is not simply that roles conflict in terms of time (or indeed that they conflict in terms of opposite purposes) but that there are too many roles for one person to handle, is not confined to law firms. It was recognised by Handy,[8] and indeed he identified the transition from executive to manager as a classic instance of its onset. The problem is however magnified by the partnership structure, with its mixture of ownership and management, and the often collegiate nature of its proceedings. In addition, as with any professional service firm, the partner does not just direct 'production' (the delivery of services) by others but is also himself a front-line producer. If this induces stresses with which he cannot cope (and both he and those around him should be alert for signs of the problem), co-operative rather than unilateral efforts will be required to address the situation. It will be necessary to analyse the relative importance of the roles, attribute priorities to them, consider delegation where possible, and to construct a working pattern which can accommodate the results of those efforts.

Notes

1   Mayson, S. (1997) *Making Sense of Law Firms*, Blackstone Press, para 40.1.
2   This element of his definition, i.e. 'wholly owned by lawyers', may have to change if proposals which have been approved by the Council of the Law Society, to allow solicitors to supply legal services to the public as employees of non-lawyers, are actually implemented.
3   Mayson, S. (1997) *Making Sense of Law Firms*, Blackstone Press, para 5.5.3.
4   One of the two firms which merged to form Clifford Chance LLP (as it now is), one of the biggest law firms in the world, was Clifford Turner. Its founder, the eponymous Harry Clifford Turner, was an ambulance-chasing personal injury lawyer who had much success in making claims against the companies running the then new-fangled invention, the omnibus. Indeed, so successful was he that the omnibus companies decided to protect themselves by instructing him. They went on to ask him to deal with commercial matters and the rest, as they say, is history!
5   What Mintzberg refers to as 'crafted strategy': Mintzberg, H. (1989) *Mintzberg on Management Inside Our Strange World of Organizations*, Free Press.
6   The finance director of one of the City's 'Big Four' firms once told the author that the firm's biggest single problem was retaining qualified staff. It seemed that, no matter how lavish their salaries, or how challenging the work, the demands put upon such staff were so at odds with their external needs that, at any one time, 40 per cent or more were actively looking to leave.
7   The Solicitors' Indemnity Fund Fourteenth Annual Report, in 2001, identified 326 firms as having suffered frauds by partners which had led to claims and reserves totalling £132.7m, whereas 265 firms had suffered fraud by employees leading to claims and reserves totalling only £44.7m.
8   Handy, C. (1993) *Understanding Organizations*, 4th edn, Penguin at p. 67.

2

Business structures

This chapter takes a look at the various structures which are now open to law firms, i.e. not just traditional partnerships, but also limited companies, and the new option of limited liability partnerships. It considers the pros and cons of each of these, with particular emphasis on their implications for new partners. It also reviews the possible introduction and impact of multi-disciplinary practices, and of the provision of legal services to the public by solicitors employed by companies funded and controlled from outside the legal profession.

Introduction

The structures currently permitted

Traditionally, in the UK, any solicitors' practice having more than one principal has practised as a partnership, operating under the Partnership Act 1890, or according to its own partnership deed or agreement. Similar provisions have applied in all common law jurisdictions. In 1991 the Solicitors' Incorporated Practice Rules 1988 came into force, and it became possible for solicitors to practise as a limited company. On 6 April 2001 the Limited Liability Partnerships Act 2000 (the LLP Act) came into force, and since that date it has been possible for solicitors to practise as a limited liability partnership (LLP).

However, in recent years, particularly in the light of the trend towards globalisation, there has been increasing pressure for a change in the rules to allow solicitors to be able to practise alongside those from other professions, and lawyers from other countries. The Law Society has indicated its wish to move towards multi-disciplinary partnerships (MDPs). Some major accountancy firms have launched their own associated law firms. Many overseas law firms, from both the USA and Europe, have moved into the UK, either by merger or association with UK firms, or by establishing offices in their own right and registering as foreign lawyers with the Law Society.

A new partner's considerations

In short, the landscape has changed immensely in the last decade, and it behoves any aspiring partner to consider whether the firm he is considering joining has, or is moving towards, the structure which offers the best opportunity for business development and, just as importantly, the structure which will provide the greatest protection for him as an individual.

Partnerships

The place of tradition

It is still the case that the vast majority of UK solicitors' firms, other than sole practitioners, conduct their business through the vehicle of a partnership. Much is made of the ethos of partnership, and the need for the inter-dependence of partners. Many firms still carry that theory to the extreme of not having a partnership agreement at all, relying on the 1890 Act and the idea that, if the situation reaches the point where it is necessary to get the partnership agreement out of the safe, it is too late anyway. In many instances, firms are still small enough for the theory of the personal relationship[1] of partnership to be a reality.

The growth of partnerships

For many, however, the reality is that their firms have grown to the extent that partners may not even be known to each other, and where the partnership as a whole meets perhaps only once or twice a year. In some firms, partner numbers are measured in hundreds. Is partnership still the appropriate vehicle for such firms? Clearly, the government does not think so, since one of its avowed reasons for the introduction of the LLP was its concern over the difficulties faced by the larger firms trying to operate under the partnership umbrella (see p. 23 below).

Checking the partnership agreement

As mentioned above, some firms deliberately do not have a partnership agreement. Others may well have an agreement, but one which makes no provision for the effect of taking on new members. If the agreement is not amended to record the introduction of new partners, this may create considerable scope for dispute about the effect of the document, and whether or not it continues to govern the partnership's affairs, or whether the firm has accidentally become a partnership at will under the 1890 Act, with the possibility of immediate dissolution at the whim of any one partner. It is suggested very strongly that it is in the interests of all concerned –

existing partners as well as new – to avoid the perils of that position, by arranging for a suitable agreement to be drawn up, and signed, before the day that a new partner is introduced.

Personal liability for partners

The Solicitors' Indemnity Fund

A fundamental change to partners' exposure to personal liability came into play in September 2000, with the demise of the Solicitors' Indemnity Fund and the introduction of open market insurance. Under the terms of the old Solicitors' Indemnity Fund policy, run-off cover for life was included within the policy. Thus those insured under that policy were protected, without further payment, against the risk that negligence claims, for which they were jointly and severally liable, might come to light many years after they had ceased to be partners.[2]

Current run-off cover availability

Now, however, the minimum terms which any approved insurer must include within its indemnity cover do not require such a run-off provision and, not surprisingly, insurers have not rushed to offer it as a free extra. (One insurer quoted an extra premium of twice the standard premium if it were to include such cover.) The consequence is that run-off is only available so long as there is a 'successor practice',[3] which continues to pay its premiums. This is serious enough for it to be suggested that sole practitioners, who did not consider that they would be able to sell their practices to successor firms, should retire on 31 August 2000 rather than risk subsequent exposure. Any partner in a post-2000 environment needs to know that, if he leaves the partnership at any stage, his partners have a positive obligation to continue to pay the insurance premiums while the practice continues, and to ensure that provision is made for what should happen if the practice ceases altogether. Clearly, that can only be effected through the medium of the partnership agreement. Any new partner who joins without such an agreement in place is therefore gambling that his erstwhile partners will continue in practice and insured – and the stakes are potentially enormous.

The partnership agreement

Any well-drawn partnership agreement will cover a multitude of topics, dealing with all aspects of the business's administration and governance.[4]

There are, however, a number of aspects to which a new partner should be particularly alert. He may or may not have a real influence on these at the time of admission, although the chances are greater if, as often happens, it is the fact of admission that prompts the preparation of the agreement in the first place. Even if that is not the case, he should consider whether any of the provisions are such as to dissuade him from entering the partnership, or whether any may be worthy of his future attention when he has more influence within the partnership.

The list (which reflects many of the matters in Chapters 7 and 8) is not exhaustive, but would include:

- Expectations as to capital introduction.
- Payment of interest on capital.
- Remuneration structure.
- Provision for revaluation of assets (e.g. freeholds):
  - periodically; and
  - on retirement.
- Governance and voting structures.
- Expulsion:
  - reasons for expulsion;
  - expulsion without cause; and
  - appeal procedure.
- Notice to withdraw/retire:
  - duration;
  - expiry date; and
  - 'garden leave'.
- Termination for ill health and linked insurances.
- Payment out provisions:
  - calculation process;
  - whether goodwill and work in progress are to be valued on payment out;
  - if so, the valuation process to be applied;
  - when payments are to be made;
  - what security is available; and
  - what interest is payable.
- Restrictive covenants:
  - non-solicitation;
  - non-competition; and
  - radius and duration.
- Post-withdrawal professional indemnity insurance cover.

Limited companies

Practising through a limited company

As mentioned above, it has been possible since 1991 for solicitors to practise through the medium of a limited company. The enabling statute was the Administration of Justice Act 1985,[5] but it was not until the passing of the Solicitors' Incorporated Practice Rules 1988 and their coming into force three years later that this became a reality for firms. Many solicitors remain unaware of this possibility, and of the opportunities it offers. Only a handful of practices have been registered with the Law Society (see below) and of those some have been start-ups, rather than existing partnerships converting to limited status.

Recognition by the Law Society

The Rules referred to above, now updated as the Solicitors' Incorporated Practice Rules 2001, provide that any solicitors' practice wishing to operate as a limited company must become a 'recognised professional body' before commencing operation. In most cases, however, this is not an onerous task. The chief requirement is that all participating solicitors must enter into pro forma personal guarantees of the business's potential liability to the Compensation Fund. Many solicitors appear to believe that they are required personally to guarantee *all* the firm's liabilities – which would in many ways defeat the object of the exercise – but this is not true. There are minor additional requirements for top-up professional indemnity insurance, but many firms will wish to take additional cover anyway. Likewise, there are fees payable, but these are negligible. The main factor which may be perceived as a drawback by some is that all directors and shareholders must be solicitors,[6] and so no external equity capital can be invested (see p. 22 below).

Personal liabilities in a company practice

The principal attraction of practising as a company is of course the limitation of personal liability for all but the Compensation Fund. Other exceptions are if personal guarantees are, in practice, required by, e.g. lenders or landlords, and if there is sufficient connection between a wrongful or negligent act or omission and an individual to make that individual liable to a third party (see p. 26 below). Apart from that, there are merely the possibilities which apply to anyone in the scenario of an insolvent company, e.g. wrongful trading, fraudulent trading etc.[7]

Advantages of a corporate structure

Another perceived advantage is the ability to structure the business in a fully corporate manner, with a board of directors responsible for the management of the firm. In the case of larger practices, this may well be a closer reflection of the operational requirements of the business than maintaining the fiction of participation by all partners, subject to the actions of management committees etc. Further, the ability to provide a more flexible capital structure, and to use shares as incentives under bonus schemes etc., will mirror more closely the commercial world, with which many firms are, in effect, competing for top quality staff.

Disadvantages of a company practice

One residual disadvantage is the regulatory restriction. At present, only solicitors may hold equity capital in an incorporated practice (see p. 21 above). The opportunity to use the company structure as a means to attract equity investment from third parties, for instance, so as to meet the increasingly capital-intensive demands of IT systems, is thus denied to practices. Further, the restrictions on fee sharing with non-solicitors prevent some forms of debt-related financing, such as factoring arrangements, which would be open to normal commercial enterprises.[8]

The corporate tax regime

Another area of disadvantage has been the difference between the tax regimes applying to partnerships and to companies. In particular, the change from the former to the latter used to attract a large tax charge as a result of the different treatments of work in progress (WIP). This meant that any partnership which incorporated would suffer a 'one-off' charge to tax on the difference between its valuation of WIP (which could be nil if it traded on the cash basis), and a fully valued figure for WIP on the company accounting basis of the lesser of cost and realisable value. This effect has, however, to some extent been mitigated by the provisions of the self assessment tax regime,[9] which has effected this change for partnerships, although partners' WIP is still not taxed, and conversion would lead to a charge to tax in respect of that element. Conversely, there can be advantages to a corporate structure, especially if retained profit will be needed for investment in coming years. Such retained profit would only be taxed at the reduced rate applicable under the corporation tax regime, whereas in a partnership profit is fully taxed when it is earned, rather than when it is distributed.

Accounting and audit requirements

Another aspect of operating as a company, which may be unattractive, is the obligation to have accounts fully audited and to disclose the accounting position of the business and, to an extent, the directors. This is discussed in more detail in the context of LLPs at p. 25.

Balancing the choice between a company and a partnership

A powerful factor leading to the formation of so few limited practices is simply ignorance of the option available. Another has been the major tax disincentive. Although that has now largely disappeared, there are still some benefits to a partnership-style tax structure. Beyond that, however, is still the view that the partnership ethos is more appropriate to professional practice, and that lawyers do not like the concept of yielding control to a board. Nonetheless, it can offer considerable advantages, and a would-be partner, especially in a corporate-minded firm, would do well to raise queries as to whether consideration has been given to making the change.

Limited liability partnerships

The basis of LLPs

An LLP[10] is essentially a hybrid. Like a company, it is a separate legal entity, and a body corporate. Again, just like a company, the personal liability of the participators in the business is basically limited to the investment that they have made into it, and does not extend to their personal assets. It is however open to the 'members' (the counterpart of 'partners') to conduct themselves as if they were a partnership, and they will be taxed as if they were partners. The operation will need to be recognised by the Law Society as if it were a company (see p. 21 above).

Reasons for the introduction of LLPs

In the explanatory notes to the Limited Liability Partnerships Bill, the government offered five reasons why it had decided to introduce the concept of LLPs, as follows:

- increasing frequency and size of professional negligence claims;
- depersonalising increases of numbers of partners within firms;
- increasing specialisation of partnerships;
- merging of different professions within a firm; and
- personal risks when claims exceed assets and insurance cover.

The more cynical might take the view that what the government was concerned to do was to prevent the Big-5 accountants from incorporating out of the jurisdiction (some of them had already supported the Jersey legislature in devising a limited liability partnership law) with the resultant drop in tax revenue which would result.

The opportunities offered by LLPs

Whatever the real reasons behind its introduction, the fact is that the vehicle of an LLP is now open to any partnership. The most powerful incentive for change is simply the ability for solicitors to limit their personal liability. There is no doubt that the frequency and size of possible negligence claims are a real fear for many, but they are not by any means the only likely cause of the liabilities of the business exceeding its assets. Events such as successful discrimination claims (where insurance is extremely expensive, and will not be available to those without adequate safeguards in their systems) could wipe out many firms. Straightforward trading losses are not unknown either, particularly for High Street firms with decreasing revenue and increased public expectations. Put simply, if a business can limit its members' personal exposure, it must surely make sense to do so unless there are powerful disincentives.

The tax position of LLPs

In contrast to the position with limited companies, there can be, for most partnerships, little disincentive[11] in tax terms operating against the idea of their conversion to LLPs, since their tax treatment after conversion will be the same as before.[12] Thus:

- Income tax will continue to be levied on the individual members' personal shares of the LLP's profit, as if they were trading as partners.
- Class 4 NIC contributions will be payable by members as if they were partners.
- For capital gains tax purposes all assets (while the LLP continues to trade) will be deemed to be held by them as partners, and all disposals will be by the members as partners.
- For all inheritance tax purposes the position remains as if the members were partners, so all reliefs are preserved.
- No stamp duty is payable on transfers from the partnership to the LLP, provided transfers are effected within a year of incorporation, and the underlying beneficial ownership of the assets does not change.

The governance of LLPs

The LLP Act creates a class of member called a 'designated member'. It does not however provide a definition of such members, but merely places certain administrative duties upon them, e.g. notifying changes in members' details to, or filing accounts at, Companies House. Further, not only is it possible for all members to be designated members, but that is the default position. In other words, LLPs can make as much or as little of this differentiation in status as they wish. Their structure and governance is intended to be established by agreement between the members and the LLP, which may be express or implied. In the absence of any agreement there is a short code of default provisions,[13] but it is suggested this is in many ways inadequate and even dangerous.[14] LLP partnership agreements, building onto normal partnership agreements but adding the special features required by the LLP Act, can readily be devised by firms.[15]

Corporate treatment of LLPs

Much of the effect of the LLP Act and its regulations is to apply to LLPs, in suitably adapted form, many provisions from other statutes, principally the Companies Act 1985 and the Insolvency Act 1986. Between them, those two statutes make up three of the four Schedules to the regulations which apply to LLPs in England and Wales.[16] These statutes effectively treat LLPs for accounting, auditing and insolvency purposes as if they were companies.

Disclosure of members' finances

It is important to note that the accounts of the LLP are a public document, and there are elements of disclosure of members' finances. The depth of disclosure depends on whether any of a number of exemptions are available to the LLP, according to its size.[17] Disclosure is however, in almost all cases, related to the aggregate financial position of the members' investment in the business, rather than being on an individual basis. The underlying intention is to allow the public the protection of knowing to what extent the members' ostensible belief in the solvency of the enterprise is matched by their willingness to invest their own funds in it, rather than to provide details of how much an individual member takes home each month.

There will, however, be reluctance in some partnerships to allow even this degree of disclosure, and a mystique about the privacy of the partnership accounts still exists. In recent years, however, there have been breaches in this wall. For some time, many of the largest accountants have published full corporate-style annual reports, which have included their accounts. Their partners do not seem to have suffered unduly. Also, in the professional press, 'league tables' of the top firms' respective financial positions have appeared for some years. Many feel it would be better to publish the true facts, rather than being vulnerable to the mixture of information and guesswork underlying such tables.

The 'clawback' provision

Similarly, much has been made of the provision[18] whereby, if an LLP becomes insolvent, a court may order members to repay any monies withdrawn by them in the two years before insolvency, unless they can satisfy the court that at the time of withdrawal they neither knew nor ought reasonably to have known that the LLP was or would become technically insolvent, or reasonably believed that insolvent liquidation could be avoided, e.g. by trading out of the difficulties. It is suggested however that to use this provision as a reason for not transferring to LLP status is to overlook the fact that, as a partner, the individual is fully liable, to the extent of all his assets, without any time limit applying and without the statutory defences open to a member of an LLP. In other words, while the clawback provision may be undesirable, it still leaves a member in a better position than a partner would be.

Residual personal liability

The LLP Act does not completely eliminate the possibility of an individual member remaining liable for a wrongful or negligent act or omission, in just the same way as this may apply to a director in a limited company context, or indeed an employee in either scenario. The bad news is that the practical extent of this is largely unknown, and will develop through case law. Two contrasting approaches have so far commended themselves to the House of Lords, giving respectively broad[19] and narrow[20] interpretations of when an individual may be so liable, co-extensively with the corporate body. The good news is that it appears that the insurance industry will cover this personal element of risk in the same policy as that of the LLP's risk, and without extra charge, since they regard the event as giving rise to only one risk. Thus, all but the 'offending' individual have the security of knowing that their personal assets are not at risk, and even that individual has available to him such insurance cover as is offered to the firm.

The timing of change

Stamp duty implications

There are two powerful arguments for effecting and completing any change to an LLP *before* any new partners join the strength. The first is that, under s.12 of the LLP Act, any change in the underlying personnel who constitute the partners in the partnership and the members in the LLP, and who are thus considered to be the beneficial owners of any property being transferred by the partnership or its nominees to the LLP, may jeopardise fulfilment of the conditions found in that section. Hence this may remove the ability to rely on the exemption from duty granted by that section, leading to an otherwise avoidable charge to duty. It is in the best interests of all concerned to avoid this situation.

Personal peace of mind

The other aspect, however, is for the sole benefit of the incoming partner. If he becomes a partner in a business which then converts to LLP status, there will be a period during which he will have joint and several personal liability for the debts of that partnership, including the possibility of future negligence claims. Reference has been made above to the increasing difficulties which are faced with regard to such claims, with the withdrawal of automatic run-off cover and attempts by the courts[21] to emasculate the protection offered by the Limitation Act 1980 (as amended by the Latent Damages Act 1986). If, on the other hand, the business is converted into an LLP before the new individual joins, he will *never* have to shoulder that liability, or face that risk. No matter how many years later the claim emerges, or what the insurance position is, if the claim arose before the transfer, he has no potential liability.

Implications of the choice of business vehicle

The management structure of a partnership

The basic management model which is familiar to solicitors is that of the partnership, where each partner has a voice in the management of the business. The Partnership Act 1890[22] states that each partner is entitled to take part in that management. From that starting point, firms may, according to their size, operational requirements, and culture, have delegated authority to a variety of committees, management boards, etc. Although partners may have equal or unequal votes, all partners are likely to have a say in at least the major decisions to be taken by the firm, e.g. opening or closing offices, appointing new partners, appointing the managing partner, etc. Thus the starting point is that power resides in the hands of all parties, and it is up to them how much of that they may choose to vest in their fellow partners.

The management structure of an LLP

Similar considerations will apply to LLPs. Again, the default provision[23] is to the effect that all members may take part in the management of the LLP. True, there is the separate status of 'designated member' as referred to above, but this can be either circumvented by allowing all members to be designated, or used in the same process of delegation as applies to partnerships.

The management structure of a limited company

In companies, however, it is unlikely that all the participating solicitors will be directors. Those who are not will presumably only have the residual powers vested in shareholders by company law generally – essentially the power to fire the directors. That may appear to be a major step from the ethos of partnership, but in reality the differences may be more apparent than actual. The largest partnerships already have the power to expel poorly performing partners, and the only reality of partners' control is, just as it is for shareholders, the negative power of voting at the AGM.

Capital structure of partnerships and LLPs

Once again, there will be close parallels between the structure, in capital terms, of partnerships and LLPs. Partners' or members' interests in the capital of the enterprise will consist of introduced capital, if required of them, and retained profit. They may or may not be entitled to interest on that capital. On leaving the firm, consideration will need to be given to whether there are any adjustments needed to the capital accounts to reflect revaluations of assets, e.g. if the valuations of any properties owned have not been brought up to date. That aside, the only major additional question will be whether any payments are due by way of goodwill – although that is a much less prevalent feature than it used to be. The only effective way of taking the money out of the firm (assuming that it is not to be wound up) is effectively an internal market, whereby existing or incoming partners buy out the outgoing person's share, perhaps over a period of time.

Capital structure of a limited company

In the company scenario, things will look rather different. Money initially invested by the participants will take the form of either share capital, with a nominal value attributed to it, or loan capital, with or without interest payable on it and terms agreed as to its repayment. The equivalent of interest on any share capital element will be the possibility (but not the certainty) of dividends. Retained profit will not directly impact upon the individual's entitlement. On leaving (again, assuming no winding up) it will be necessary to agree what the shares are worth. A number of imprecise factors will normally enter into a share valuation, e.g. the amount of retained profit, the view of future prospects, the impact of any under or overvaluation of assets, the discount to be attributed to a minority shareholding, etc. In theory, shares are a more marketable commodity than interests in an LLP or partnership, but in practice that option will be constrained both by the memorandum and articles of association, and by the requirements for all shareholders to be solicitors. Again, therefore, there will be only an internal market for shares, which tends to confer a disadvantage on the seller. For all these reasons, it is suggested that if a practice is configured as a limited company there should be a carefully constructed shareholders' agreement in place, governing the circumstances in which, and the pricing principles by which, shareholders can dispose of their holdings.

Possible future developments

The general background

A number of fundamental changes as to the nature of the vehicle by which legal and other professional services may be delivered to the public have been made in recent years. Depending on the chosen market place of his firm, a new partner may need to be acutely conscious of the threats – or opportunities – that such measures offer. The debate has taken place against a complex backdrop of pressure from bodies such as the Office of Fair Trading, which seeks to encourage competition for the delivery of legal services, and the various professional bodies (especially the Law Society) which are concerned lest relaxation of regulatory regimes weakens public protection and their own ability to operate as regulators. Recently, the debate has been thrown into sharp focus by the consultation paper 'In the Public Interest' issued by the Lord Chancellor's Department (the LCD). At the time of writing, the outcome of that consultation is awaited.

Authorised institutions

One of the options being considered is that certain institutions might be authorised by the government to conduct two specific types of business, namely conveyancing and probate work. Legislation already exists which would enable the government to do this (i.e. the Courts and Legal Services Act 1990) but this legislation was formulated in the heat of the conveyancing boom of the late 1980s and, after that rush subsided, it was presumably not considered necessary to use the power. This possibility has now, however, been reintroduced to the legal landscape by the LCD. Partners coming into firms with heavy emphasis on these types of business should be aware of the threat that such authorisation might bring, as those institutions likely to win approval, e.g. banks, would have none of the capital constraints that face most solicitors' firms in equipping and staffing major departments.

Multi-disciplinary partnerships

Another possibility is the introduction of the Multi-Disciplinary Partnership (MDP). Here, the idea is that different professions can come together within one business unit. However, there are two main arguments against allowing MDPs. First, there is the question of who should regulate such bodies. Second, there is the fear (particularly in post-Enron days) that the commercial reality of such partnerships will bring pressures that will be inimical to proper professionalism and act against the public interest. Solicitors could be instructed by their bosses to act in ways which would maximise profit but might not be for the benefit of their clients. In this country,[24] the Law Society has approved a model whereby the majority of partners would need to be solicitors, and the whole firm would have to be regulated by the Law Society. Other partners would not be required to be from any particular profession, so the door would be open for firms to take their senior support staff into partnership, as well as other professionals. The idea has however hit a snag, in that counsel has advised that primary legislation would be needed in order to enable the Law Society to regulate non-solicitors and, so far, the LCD has shown no sign of heeding the Law Society's request for the necessary allocation of Parliamentary time.

Provision of legal services by non-legal companies

In the meantime, the Law Society approved a further idea in March 2002. This suggestion is that solicitors could be employed by companies owned and controlled by non-lawyers, but without the current restriction that they can only supply legal services to their employer and staff colleagues. In other words, they could supply services to the general public. This has become known by the shorthand name of 'Tesco Law', although it is not necessarily the supermarkets which would be the only ones bidding to take over areas of work in this way. There are two major objections. One is that this will harm the provision of publicly funded legal work, as those firms which practise mainly in areas vulnerable to competition from such institutions are also those who would be doing publicly funded work, and their ability to survive may be affected. The second is that the public protection afforded by existing regulatory regimes could not be replicated. The Law Society's consent was subject to the establishment of public safeguards equal to those currently offered by solicitors. An inability to formulate such suggestions has meant that the scheme has made little real progress to date, but it is always possible that the result of the LCD's survey may be to take any decisions out of the profession's hands. Any partner coming into a firm that would be vulnerable to an attack like this should carefully review what alternative strategies the firm may have in place to protect its future viability in such circumstances.

Notes

1 Partnership Act 1890, s.1(1).
2 See **note 21** (p. 32) as to modern cases affecting this potential liability.
3 As defined each year in the Solicitors' Indemnity Rules.
4 It is not the place of this work to serve as a guide to such agreements. For readers who are not familiar with such agreements, reference should be made to the current volume on 'Partnerships' in Butterworths' *Encyclopaedia of Forms and Precedents*.
5 Sections 9, 10 and Sched. 2.
6 Or members of another category of lawyers accepted by Rules 3 and 4 of the Solicitors Incorporated Practice Rules 2001, i.e. barristers, Registered European Lawyers, Registered Foreign Lawyers, or non-registered European Lawyers (as defined).
7 Insolvency Act 1986, ss.213 and 214.
8 The giving of debentures may be regarded as acceptable if there is a provision to the effect that if receivers are appointed at least one of them must be a solicitor so as to enable debts to be collected without breaching confidentiality rules.
9 Introduced by various Finance Acts from 1994 onwards.
10 As to LLPs generally, see Armour, D. (2001) *Limited Liability Partnerships – the new legislation*, Tolleys, which offers a short explanatory text, and, most importantly, not only the text of the LLP Act and its accompanying regulations but also annotated versions of the various statutes incorporated by that legislation as they are amended by it. See also Young, S. (2001) *Limited Liability Partnerships Handbook*, Tolleys, for a more detailed textual analysis of the subject, a draft LLP partnership agreement, and the guidance notes produced by the Law Society for the specific application of the legislation to solicitors.
11 The only significant disadvantage for most will be a requirement to bring into their accounts the overhead element of members' work in progress. One group of firms for whom conversion may not be sensible, however, is those with existing annuity commitments (whether current or contingent) as, even if these are profit related, they will need to be valued annually and shown as a liability in the balance sheet. See the Statement of Recommended Practice issued in May 2001 by the Consultative Committee of Accountancy Bodies.
12 Limited Liability Partnerships Act 2000, ss.10–12.
13 Limited Liability Partnership Regulations 2001, SI 2001/1090, regs. 7 and 8.
14 See Young, S. (2001) *Limited Liability Partnerships Handbook*, Tolleys, Chapter 8.

15   Ibid, Appendix 4.
16   See Armour, D. (2001) *Limited Liability Partnerships – the new legislation*, Tolleys.
17   See Young, S. (2001) *Limited Liability Partnerships Handbook*, Tolleys, Chapter 11.
18   Section 214A of the Insolvency Act 1986, as inserted by Sched. 3 to the Limited Liability Partnership Regulations 2001, SI 2001/1090.
19   *Smith* v. *Bush* [1990] 1 AC 837; *Caparo* v. *Dickman* [1990] 2 AC 605 each of which adopted a tripartite test of foreseeability, proximity, and whether it was just and reasonable to impose a duty of care.
20   *Williams* v. *Natural Life Health Foods Ltd* [1998] 1 WLR 830, which proposed a different test relating to the extents to which the individual had assumed personal liability for the negligent advice given, and the claimant had both relied upon that personal assumption and acted reasonably in so doing. For a discussion as to the relative merits of these tests see Evans, H. (2002) *Lawyers' Liabilities*, 2nd edn., Sweet & Maxwell.
21   Fortunately, the House of Lords in *Cave* v. *Robinson, Jarvis* & *Rolf* [2002] 2 All ER 641 (disapproving the earlier decision in *Brocklesby* v. *Armitage* & *Guest* [2001] 1 All ER 172) appears to be attempting to draw a line in the sand against efforts to erode the principle of limitation to the point of its disappearance.
22   Section 24(5).
23   Limited Liability Partnership Regulations 2001, SI 2001/1090, reg. 7(3).
24   The idea of MDPs has met with mixed reception abroad. The American Bar Association, in 1999, voted against a proposal which would have allowed them, but did not close the door if public protection could be ensured. Some states may be going their own way, however. In Australia the climate is more favourable, and at least one state, New South Wales, has approved a law permitting MDPs. Canada is in favour in principle, but New Zealand has decided to wait and see what mistakes others make first! In Europe, the ECJ decided in the *Wouters* case (Case C-309/99) that it was not unlawful for the Dutch Bar to have laid down in 1993 a rule that members could only enter into a partnership with others whose profession's primary purpose was the practice of law, as it was possible for this to be considered as being reasonable for the proper regulation of the profession.

3

Systematic management

This chapter takes an overall look at various management systems, whether they describe themselves as 'quality management', 'risk management', or 'case management'. Existing systems which offer external certification of a firm's systems are discussed, in terms of their background, application, and future development. These are then linked to the fundamental concepts of risk control, and the development of experience in the open market professional indemnity insuance world. The role and design of case management systems are considered. The chapter goes on to look at the challenges which all such systems bring. Finally, it offers a summary of what new partners should be looking for in terms of their firm's approach to and implementation of systematic management; and what firms will be looking at when examining the records of potential partners in respect of their attitude to and compliance with such systems.

General

Introduction

From the early 1990s onwards, lawyers have been bombarded with various options for the introduction of systems offering miracle cures for all their management ills. There have been competing 'quality' standards – Lexcel (a.k.a. the Law Society's Practice Management Standards), ISO 9000 (formerly BS 5750), Barmark, Investors in People, the Legal Aid Franchise Quality Assurance Standard (LAFQAS) (now the Community Legal Service Specialist Quality Mark), etc. The development of risk management as a concept has been driven by the dawning, in the late 1990s, in the wake of the property slump in the early part of the decade, of an awareness of the horrendous consequences of the poor standard of work then carried out. IT suppliers have marketed their case management systems as the panacea to all of an overworked firm's ills. Few have put the pieces of the jigsaw together, and offered a holistic approach to the overall problem, and opportunities, that systematic management offers.

Terminology

In this chapter the overall term 'systematic management' has been quite deliberately chosen, partly to encompass the three elements of quality, risk and case management, and partly because of the shortcomings of the existing terms, and their lack of inter-relationship. 'Systematic management' is intended to offer a joined-up view of the ways in which providing a skeleton of steps to be taken throughout a firm's operations can give the best opportunity for the individual lawyers to put flesh on the bones. The usual terms, and their drawbacks, are as below.

- 'Quality' is a term with which many lawyers feel uncomfortable, since it does not reach into what they consider to be the heart of their work, and affect the quality of their legal advice and direct fee-earning work.
- 'Risk management', especially in the aftermath of the fiasco of the Solicitors' Indemnity Fund shortfall, is often interpreted by lawyers as purely the avoidance of negligence claims. This ignores all other aspects of the concept of controlling the totality of those risks which affect a law firm.
- 'Case management' is a term which has been used to cover the many different systems offered by IT suppliers, which may vary from the hopelessly overcomplicated to systems which are so inflexible as to be virtually unusable.

Existing 'quality' systems

Overview

There is more similarity than dissimilarity between existing systems, because the fundamental concept which underlies them all is the same, namely that a firm should design a system for its activities which will comply with standards pre-set by an external body, and which will be suitable for the firm. Some (e.g. Lexcel) apply to all the firm's activities, and some concentrate, although not necessarily exclusively, on one aspect either of management (e.g. human resource issues for Investors in People) or output (e.g. publicly funded work for the LSC's Specialist Quality Mark). It is useful to know what each of these standards has to offer, and what their shortcomings are.

ISO 9000

Background

ISO 9000 is the foundation of most of the systems on offer, and has been around since 1979. Introduced to the legal profession in the early 1990s, it was originally known as BS 5750, but later changed to the international equivalent. The standard was initially designed for general application to industry, and so translating it into service-industry terms, and then law firm terms in particular, was no easy task. Nonetheless it could be done, and the first solicitors' firm was registered in 1991. At that time, part of the motivation was the expectation that institutional clients, especially those in the governmental and quasi-governmental fields, would before long require their service suppliers to be registered as part of their own quality compliance procedures. This underlay Klafter and Walker's work[1] in 1995, which took as its theme the suggestion that any firm not so registered would lose all work of this nature.

Development in the legal profession

However, in practice only a very few institutional clients have required such certification. ISO 9000 has thus lost its main selling point, and that, combined with the difficulties in applying a system which is not designed specifically for use by law firms, has meant that only a few firms (mostly in response to the occasional client pressures mentioned above) have obtained and maintained ISO 9000 certification. A new version of this standard has recently been launched, with the 2001 version of the family of documents which together make up the 9000 standard. It is designed to be more user-friendly, and to concentrate more on outcomes than initial procedural requirements. Despite this, the general view seems to be that the ISO have missed the boat as far as UK law firms are concerned, in the light of the developments which have occurred within more specific standards.

Investors in People

Background

Another well-established standard, and again one which has undergone a recent facelift, is the government sponsored Investors in People standard (IIP), administered by a dedicated company. The IIP award itself was launched in 1990, but its roots go back a lot further than that. The requirements of the system have in effect been carried forward from the now almost entirely defunct Industrial Training Boards, set up in the 1960s. They are, in effect, the government's view of what constitutes scientific management of a firm. Again, they are not law firm-specific, but since the standards concentrate on human resource issues, they are easier to adapt to a legal scenario than ISO 9000.

Development

Further, the latest version of this standard tests compliance less by evidence of written procedures than by verbal examination of staff, in order to discover whether the 12 indicators are actually being observed and/or implemented. This shift to consideration of outcomes rather than documentation sits well with other standards, e.g. Lexcel, as the one standard can be regarded as testing the design of a system, and the other standard as testing its product, at least in a specific area. A number of firms have therefore found it desirable to combine certification to two standards, especially as cost savings can be made by using one assessment visit to cover both. Other advantages to IIP are that it has – so far at least – the highest public recognition of any of the available standards. It is often a pathway to generous government funding for a wide range of training activities, including management training. It is also expanding in scope: in January 2003 a Leadership and Management module was launched and a 'Work-Life Balance Model is to follow.

LAFQAS / CLS Specialist Quality Mark

Background

The other instance of government influence in the development of system requirements for law firms has been the role of the Legal Aid Board, latterly the Legal Services Commission (LSC), in promoting its own standards for firms that wish to offer legal aid or publicly funded work. When the Board initially introduced its franchising standards in the early 1990s, this was the first such scheme to be launched by a government anywhere. Gradually, compliance with this standard has become a prerequisite for firms wishing to practise in this arena. In parallel with this, however, have been increasingly stringent financial qualifications for those seeking public funding, an increasing number of non-lawyer agencies being brought within the LSC's net, and a reduction of the areas where public funding is available.

Development to date

Firms that practise in areas like crime, family or immigration have become increasingly dependent on being able to meet this standard. However, the standard has become marginalised for firms that do not see their future in such areas, and do not appreciate the extremely prescriptive approach of the Commission (nor, indeed, the irony of that body, with its appalling record as to its own efficiency of process and communication with the profession, lecturing the profession on standards of business efficiency!). The standard has previously applied at two levels, namely the firm's overall management procedures (financial management, business planning, etc.) and the working practices of those involved directly in publicly funded work. It has not penetrated to areas of work such as company and commercial departments, which have remained blissfully oblivious to, for instance, the very detailed requirements as to supervision and delegation of work.

Future changes

Now, however, the LSC has indicated that it may offer to extend its audit to cover those areas. Its ostensible position is that this would be merely a service offered to firms that wish to avoid the cost of a second audit to other standards. The alternative view is that this is in fact an attempt by the Commission, as a creature of the Lord Chancellor's Department, to establish itself as the profession-wide regulatory body, to the exclusion of others.[2] The Law Society has, of late, been working with the Commission (as distinct from the formerly antagonistic stance between the two bodies) to persuade the Commission that the availability of Lexcel obviates the necessity for this. Considerable progress has been made towards passporting between the two standards in the areas where they cover common ground. (See p. 39 for the LSC's interface with the Bar Council.)

Lexcel

Background

The Law Society introduced its Practice Management Standards in 1991. They are a comprehensive code, drawing on work in adapting (as it then was) BS 5750 for law firms, and specifically designed for law firms across the spectrum. It was originally criticised for its lack of external audit, so claiming compliance was of limited value in external communications. On the other hand, firms had an opportunity to introduce the standards without external scrutiny. External audit, administered by the Law Society but conducted by independent bodies, was introduced in 1998, and the resultant award was badged as 'Lexcel'. It has six main sections, covering:

- management structure;
- services and forward planning;
- financial management;
- managing people;

- office administration; and
- case and file management.

Development to date

Since 1998,[3] 277 units have obtained certification: 184 firms in private practice; 92 local government departments; and one other. Another 62 units are undergoing assessment, and 205 units have also offered a definite commitment to working towards the attainment of the mark. Revisions to the standard were piloted in 2000 and implemented during 2001, and from October of that year all Lexcel audits are to the new version. The most telling change is in the field of risk management procedures.

Future development

It is thought that the Law Society's efforts to promote Lexcel will increase for two reasons, namely its place in the client-care imperative, and the effort to avoid being subsumed by the LSC. In client-care terms, much is concentrated on a clear and consistent delivery of service to the client, which meets the main client requirements of approachability and availability (technical expertise being almost a given in most clients' eyes[4]) and which matches the client's expectations rather than the lawyer's. The desire is to achieve the position where a client will consider it vital for a firm to hold the mark. To achieve that, it is suggested that the standard itself needs to develop more responsively, and that changes will need to be more frequent than before. Areas under discussion include:

- Adding more required elements, such as:
  - further risk management aspects;
  - regulatory issues such as data protection and money laundering; and
  - equality and diversity.

- Offering voluntary modules for firms wishing to use the standard as a business development tool,[5] such as:
  - measures of client and staff satisfaction;
  - performance management and benchmarking; and
  - effective business planning.

Barmark

The Bar's own set of standards was introduced in 1999, and is a clearly drafted code, mainly covering aspects of chambers management and communication with professional and lay clients alike. The Bar Council have also been working with the LSC and have agreed upon an adaptation of Barmark to form the 'Quality Mark for the Bar'. This was launched in September 2002, and all chambers which have Barmark (54 sets to November 2002[6]) can be passported into the new LSC mark if they agree to cover its additional requirements within a year.

Other standards

Additional sets of standards exist other than on a profession-wide basis. These may be the product of a single firm's own efforts; or may be offered by groupings of firms such as LawGroup UK, which recognise the importance of consistent standards for their member firms, but do not, for various reasons, wish to be so prescriptive as to insist on standards such as Lexcel.

Extending the scope of standards

A new development which is just starting to be mentioned in the context of professional service firms is the introduction of environmental protection standards, chiefly ISO 14000. As with ISO 9000, the protagonists aver that attainment of this standard will particularly benefit firms practising in the governmental and quasi-governmental fields. Although the validity of this proposition might be questioned, it may well be the next logical direction for firms which are up to scratch with their systems generally, and would like to be able to demonstrate their 'green' credentials for either philosophical or marketing reasons.

Risk control

Risk control as a concept

To a solicitor, the phrase risk control, or risk management, will immediately bring thoughts of their professional indemnity insurance premiums. Few will think of the myriad range of other risks that they might encounter. No list can be exhaustive, but amongst those risks which should perhaps be considered are:

- complaints as to service standards;
- non-payment or late payment by clients;
- hidden unprofitability of certain types of work;
- employment, e.g. discrimination, claims;
- damage to reputation;
- fraud;

- deliberate harm to, e.g. IT systems by disgruntled staff;
- disaster risk to premises and/or IT systems; and
- health and safety.

Solicitors' Indemnity Fund audit tool

The Solicitors Indemnity Fund (SIF) which, for 11 years until September 2000, was the only professional indemnity insurance for solicitors, did not exactly cover itself in glory in its last few years, with its failure to provide adequate reserves and reinsurance leading to a shortfall in the order of magnitude of £400m. However, shortly before its demise it published a self-audit tool, a copy of which was sent to every firm. It represents the concentrated wisdom of over 200,000 claims, and as such is the most authoritative document on where risks may lie. The queries it poses reflect the fact (astonishing to many) that only 10 per cent of all claims come from ignorance or misapplication of the law, as opposed to procedural errors, such as missing time limits, etc. Helpfully, in reflecting that wisdom through the questions which it suggests a firm should ask itself, it does not confine itself to the negligence-related aspects of the problems signposted, but also takes into account some of the other risks mentioned above. All new partners would be well advised to familiarise themselves with this document.

The common sense element

The SIF audit tool clearly demonstrates that much of the requirement for a systematic approach to risk control is the need to ensure that the collective experience and common sense of those within the firm is applied each and every time that relevant questions arise. A parallel would be a pilot's pre-take-off checklist. None of the questions on that list, of itself, are likely to be anything other than obvious to the pilot; however the checklist is designed to ensure that he asks *all* the questions *every* time.

Applying the common sense approach

A simple example is the series of questions relating to a firm's willingness to take on a new case where the client is known to have used one or more firms of solicitors on the same matter previously. The solicitor in question, like any professional, will be influenced by his belief in his own ability to do the job better than his predecessor, and his ability to control the difficult client. But, equally, he will be aware that a client who has had problems with one firm may be conditioned against the profession, capable of complaining, and just as likely to be a problem to his new lawyer. The task of the SIF tool is to force the firm to formulate a policy on the matter, and to ensure that the individual considers this policy before accepting the client. Hopefully, in this way, the comment of 'I knew from the start that this one was going to be hassle' will disappear. The difficulty of the task does not lie in identifying, or acknowledging, the nature of the problem, but in designing a system for controlling it which will not be intrusive and will fit with all other aspects of the firm's operations.

Cross-boundary risk

Lawyers like to 'pigeonhole' issues, but this is not an approach which should be adopted when considering risk control. Rather, when devising systems, firms should consider all potential aspects and risks which may attach to a particular event. Take, as an instance, the scenario set out in the box below. It may initially seem difficult to make the mental leap that the scenario illustrates: from a failure of interview procedures to financial harm; major time commitment; poor staff relations; and professional disciplinary measures, but the example shows that the chain is easy to construct. The designer of the firm's systems must recognise the importance of potential linkages, so that (in this instance) putting together a standard interview format, with potentially discriminatory elements removed and full evidential backing as to the techniques used, is given the importance it deserves.

> The firm is open to an accusation of race discrimination as a consequence of failure to appoint a particular shortlisted candidate from an ethnic minority group. Initially, this might be thought to pose a risk simply of a finding against the firm in an employment tribunal. Then, however, given the fact of potentially unlimited compensation, the partners will realise how important the matter may become to them financially (since they will almost certainly not be insured for the claim), and how much in the way of resources – in respect of time just as much as money – it is likely to take to defend the claim. After that, the potentially damaging reputational aspects of the public airing of the events surrounding the claim should be considered. There may also be harmful effects on their existing staff relations, if other employees consider there to have been discriminatory tendencies which might in future affect them. Lastly, the partners may be forced to realise that their fellow lawyers, in the form of the Solicitors' Disciplinary Tribunal, will also take a dim view of the harm that may attach to the whole profession from acts of discrimination if proved, so that disciplinary proceedings against all partners for offences under the Practice Rules may follow.

Insurance in risk control terms

Too often, insurance is thought of as the 'be all and end all' of risk control, instead of being merely a constituent (if important) part of it. A suggested sequence of events for a proper approach to risk control is set out below:

- Appoint a senior partner / manager with risk control responsibilities.
- Identify a risk.
- Investigate how it can systematically be reduced.
- Quantify the residual risk.
- Consider whether it can be insured against.
- Investigate the cost of insurance.
- Assess what part of the residual risk should economically be borne by the firm as self-insured excess.

Analysing the potential impact of the risk

Any risk falls into three bands. First, the element that the firm can, by its own efforts, reasonably expect to eliminate. Second, the portion of the residual risk which the firm cannot economically bear itself, and therefore has to lay off in terms of insurance. Third, the level of the residual risk which the firm can cover from its own normal resources, and which it therefore does not need to ask the insurer to cover, thus obtaining reduced premium levels. This shows the importance of risk control systems in a number of ways. They will initially define the expected frequency of claims against which insurance will be needed. As such, the insurer's estimate of the efficacy of those systems will be as important as the firm's, since the insurer will take that estimate into account when setting premium levels. The actual effect of the risks will be reflected in the subsequent claims record, with its own consequent effect on premium levels. Lastly, the frequency of claims will inform the firm's own decision on what levels of excess payments may be tolerable.

Open market insurance

The introduction of the open market

All of the above was thrown into the sharpest possible focus during 2000. The Solicitors' Indemnity Rules were changed to remove the monopoly which the SIF had on insuring the first tier (£1m per claim) of solicitors' negligence cover. A number of insurers, who were prepared to offer cover meeting certain minimum requirements of the Law Society, were 'approved' by the Society. Thirty-five insurers, with no track record of the market sector (although, in many cases, with ex-SIF staff who did have such experience) set out to offer cover to 8,500 firms, none of which had experience of negotiating such cover, all at the same time.

Initial experience of the open market

Chaos ensued, as most of the major insurers waited until the last possible minute before declaring the premium levels to be offered, lest the information be commercially useful to their rivals. Some insurers deliberately targeted certain sizes of firm. Premium levels, when eventually quoted, varied hugely. A factor of four between highest and lowest quotes was, according to anecdotal evidence, commonplace. Eventually, with the exception of those firms[7] which went into the 'Assigned Risks Pool' (a temporary-only home, at punitive rates, for those who either had not arranged cover or, more likely, had such a bad claims record that no insurer would offer cover) all firms were able to obtain insurance cover.

Lessons of the open market

Despite the chaos, there were still valuable lessons to be learned. First, in overall terms, the profession's premium payments for first-tier cover went down from, in round figures, £240m per year to £154m per year. No doubt some of that drop reflected insurers' attempts to gain market share, but logically some must also have reflected the idea that the profession was in better shape – i.e. a better risk – than it had been. Second, there was a considerable emphasis on firms' risk control procedures. Some insurers called for copies of firms' procedural manuals, distributed their own risk assessment questionnaires, and/or enquired whether firms had undertaken the task of going though the SIF self-audit process. A number of insurers also offered to put risk management consultants into insured firms, at the insurers' expense, to advise on changes which could profitably be made in risk control systems. However, the sub-text to this generous offer was that deficiencies found would be reported to the insurers. The insurers would then, if prepared to offer repeat cover, impose conditions as to compliance with the consultants' recommendations.

Future refinement of the open market process

In other words, the whole process became much more sophisticated than had been the case with the SIF. It took into account not only the backward-looking issue of 'burning costs' (a term indicating the annual bill to insurers for payments or reservations for claims, claimants' costs and defence costs, minus self-insured excesses); but also the forward-looking idea of the control of future claims' frequency through management systems. The result, for firms which were amongst the better organised, was savings of premium levels considerably greater than the 40 per cent average experienced across the profession. It is suggested that the importance of these increasingly individualised trends can only grow over time, particularly as insurers are called upon by successful firms to offer contracts for longer than a year, and to provide premium refunds for good claims records. The significance of this is shown by the fact that the aggregate premium level for the profession has risen to an estimated £220m for 2002/3, so all methods of reducing a firm's premium levels are vital.

Case management systems

The role of case management systems

It is not the task of this work to consider the wide range of case management systems currently on offer. Rather, consideration here is as to their generic usefulness (or otherwise) amongst the toolbox of risk control devices. Additional uses of IT, which do not form part of case management packages, may also have an important role to play in the overall systematic management concept, e.g. accounts software may automatically trigger alarms as thresholds are about to be reached on estimates given to clients for anticipated cost levels. Nor, indeed, should such measures be considered solely in the context of IT – a religiously utilised manual diary system is a much more efficient tool than an occasionally-used computer-based one.

Differing approaches to case management systems

The suggestion is that what have become generically known as 'case management systems' are of twofold effect. On the one hand, from the viewpoint of the fee earner or secretary operating the system, they are a means of undertaking the day-to-day tasks required in conducting client-facing casework in a speedier and more efficient way than would otherwise be the case. On the other hand, they may be used as a management tool, in undertaking (*inter alia*) the following tasks:

- Ensuring that the correct steps, and only the correct steps, are taken by the fee earner in each case.
- Ensuring that those steps are taken when they should be, and that time limits are not missed.
- Ascertaining, when staff are ill or on holiday, the position of each matter and what action needs to be taken.
- Controlling the caseloads of individual fee earners.
- Enabling and facilitating more efficient supervision of delegated matters or parts thereof.

The range of case management systems

Case management means many things to many people. In some instances, particularly with those types of work which lend themselves to a 'shrink wrap' or commodity approach, such as residential conveyancing, the case management system may be a fairly rigidly controlled set of steps which consists of prompting and tracking a highly predictable set of events and documents, and thus has few 'what if?' stages to cope with. It may in truth be little more than a document production system – and, if that is all that is required, it will be none the worse for that, providing this limitation is recognised.

Other systems, where the IT supplier has made a conscious decision to offer as flexible a product as possible, may have a wide range of options for coping with any situation, according to a client's preferences. However, to reach a stage where such a system is workable in practice, an enormous amount of the client firm's time must be spent in defining (sometimes for the first time) the workflow patterns of each affected type of work, precisely what standard documents will be used, and what are the options to be dealt with in the context of those patterns. Unless there are suitable dedicated staff resources, this can take years, or indeed it may present such a problem that the project is abandoned altogether.

Finding the effective solution

For systematic management purposes, the ideal lies somewhere between the above extremes. The former example is deficient, since although it is effective for moving the case itself forward, it offers none of the management control techniques bulleted above. The overflexible system may never become effectively operative at fee-earner level, and may offer such a wealth of management information that the hapless supervisor becomes afflicted by the 'paralysis of analysis'. What is required is a system which offers sufficient default settings to be usable without over-customisation, but can be adapted as experience dictates, and which will yield the managerial data required.

The human element

Role changes caused by systematic management

Initiating any sort of systematic management takes time, and often money. Consultants may have a role to play in the initial stages, even if only to ask the questions which partners should have been asking of themselves anyway. There are opportunity cost implications in the expenditure of partners' time on devising and implementing the systems. There may be both hardware and software costs involved. There will inevitably be costs of training, and these may be both direct and indirect. In short, it represents a not inconsiderable investment. It is easy to waste that investment if the requisite roles of those responsible for implementing the systems in practice, and any necessary changes in roles, are not properly performed and adjusted.

Leadership

First, the introduction of such systems needs careful leadership. Change management, and what may amount to 'business process re-engineering' (see Chapter 9) is never easy, and needs careful, planned leadership. That leadership must come from the top, and senior management must demonstrate its commitment to the concepts underlying the systems adopted, on a daily basis, or personnel will simply not accept the importance of the system's observance. Thus leadership needs to be a consistent feature, and to be reflected in a willingness to continually test the efficacy and appropriateness of the systems, to monitor the results of those tests, and to heed the lessons thus learned by adapting and improving the systems.

Monitoring use of the system

Human nature being what it is, any system will need to be monitored to ensure that all personnel affected by it are regularly and properly performing the tasks required of them. This is a different concept from supervision (see pp. 48–49). It is necessary to check that the procedural steps required by the system are actually being taken, when and in the way in which they should be. An ability to cajole a fee earner into compliance when feeling the inevitable sense of tedium that at least some procedural steps are likely to generate, is essential. It is suggested that this is a task which does not need to be – and indeed perhaps should not be – undertaken by a legally qualified fee-earner. An individual from a background where system compliance is a long-established concept, e.g. banking, insurance, etc., may be better placed to carry out this role. However, the person monitoring compliance will require the right to ask questions of everyone – from office junior to senior partner (especially, perhaps, the senior partner!) and a direct line of reporting to the top tier of management, so that any concerns are not capable of being distorted lower down the management chain. Once accepted, this role can become a highly creative one, identifying any developments needed in the system, and reporting recommendations.

Delegation

Introduction

Perhaps the most difficult role change will be for those who, under the system in question, delegate work and thus become liable for the supervision of the work of others. This may apply at a variety of levels, from department head, through a newly-appointed partner who is given responsibility for a number of fee earners, to an experienced paralegal supervising a section of, say, claims handlers. The point in each case is a simple one, and the same one, i.e. that delegation without subsequent supervision is an accident waiting to happen, and that effective supervision takes time. Lawyers are only too inclined to consider delegation as the synonym for abdication, i.e. an act of passing over a file, the day before a time limit is due to run out, allows them to heave a sigh of relief and mutter a silent prayer never to have to see it again. (There is a time when this may be an appropriate action, when as part of a risk management process an arrangement is made for the exchange of files upon which fee earners have a complete mental block, but that is an entirely different process!) In most cases, however, delegation should be a very structured process, understood by all necessary parties.

Pre-delegation considerations

Delegation is not even the first step in the chain of events. Before that can take place, the would-be delegator has to consider whether:

- the proposed delegatee has the competence to take the case, both in terms of the technical expertise and the range of personal skills required;
- the delegatee has the capacity to take the case, in view of the workload already being undertaken;
- he or another proposed supervisor has the expertise, and will have the time, to supervise the delegatee properly;
- the respective rates of remuneration of the delegatee, and payment for the work, are sufficient for it to be profitable for the firm to undertake the work at the level of delegation proposed; and
- the client will accept the delegation.

The role of file management systems

Delegation will begin with a handover of the file (or a specific task on the file) with full and clear instructions. The delegator's role is succeeded by that of the supervisor, albeit that in many cases it will fall to the same person to discharge both tasks. Here, properly constructed systems will come to the aid of everyone involved. For one thing, proper file management will allow a supervisor to establish quickly, after picking up a file, where the relevant documents may be found; what are the salient points of the file; what risk-related issues are involved (time limits, undertakings, etc.); and what stage the matter has reached. Thus he can readily see whether the file handler is coping or if, for instance, that person is away ill or on holiday, he can brief himself or another person to cover in the interim. On the other hand, a fee earner to whom a file is passed will also have ready access to the background to the task ahead of him.

Parties involved in the delegation process

Those involved may include:

- The partner effecting the delegation. He needs to be clear as to what his residual responsibilities are while the file remains with the delegatee, and when it is likely to return to his care.
- The delegatee. He needs clear and timely instructions as to the background of the file, the steps he is required to take, the lines of communication with other parties, his reporting obligations as far as the delegator is concerned, and the timescale within which actions needed to be taken.
- The client. He needs to be kept informed, as part of the firm's client-care programme, as to who is to be responsible for his file, what charging principles are to apply, and with whom he should communicate.
- The support staff involved (secretaries, etc.). They need to know who is dealing with work on the file and to whom enquiries should be referred.
- The department head (if different from the delegator partner). He must be aware of the transfer for his own supervisory and work allocation purposes.
- Other staff, for example those responsible for data inputting and the accounts department. They should be kept up to date so that every file's current status can be correctly maintained.

Supervision

The importance of good communication

During the lifespan of the operation of the delegated authority, there should be frequent opportunities for the two main parties to communicate about the matter. The amount of actual discussion will depend on factors such as the complexity of the matter, the likelihood of the client contacting the delegator with an enquiry, and so on. It is important that the channel of communication is open and known, so that each party feels easy about making any comments and asking any questions they feel to be appropriate. There may be some pre-set stages when it is agreed that there will be discussion or reporting, perhaps according to the passage of time, or according to the stage reached in the life of the matter.

The role of case management systems

Depending on the sophistication of the case management systems available to him, the supervisor may be able to conduct some of his supervision remotely. Diary systems should indicate crucial dates, preferably with a facility for automatic escalation of reminders to the supervisor, so that he will be able to see if the tasks needed are being performed in time. Even if they are, he should watch for warning signs, such as the fee earner who is always compliant, but only at the last moment. He can monitor workloads, in terms of new files taken on, overall case numbers, and hours being worked. He can see how efficient the fee earner is in his work, in economic terms, by looking at his recovery rates, and the amount of supposedly chargeable time being written off.

Giving supervision its proper priority

All this takes time, and is likely to take place against a background where the supervisor himself is under pressure from many sources – clients demanding contact, partners emphasising targets, etc. To work, two further elements are required. First, time must be allocated as part of the recognition of the supervisor's function. Second, the supervisor himself must recognise that the task is a matter of priority, and not one which he can simply move to the bottom of the pile whenever a crisis blows up. This sounds simple, but in practice it is exactly the opposite. The system which most clearly recognises this need, and is most prescriptive in its requirements, is the CLS Specialist Quality Mark. It lays down strict tests as to the supervisor's own technical ability to supervise, and imposes a strict regime of supervisory file reviews, etc. Those in more sheltered areas of work, which are not affected by the requirements of publicly funded work, have much to learn from their litgious colleagues!

Delegation and supervision – concluding the process

The end of the process of delegation for any piece of work should be just as clearly delineated and reported as its beginning. Many of the processes set out at p. 48 above should be reversed. There should be the same degree of certainty as to the fact and consequences of the closure of the process as there was to its commencement.

The control of fraud

It may seem odd to talk of accounting systems in the context of systematic management, and risk control, etc., but in fact the rules applicable to the control of the finances flowing through solicitors' firms are probably the oldest and most widespread example of such systems. Furthermore, sadly, they are sometimes the most abused, with catastrophic consequences. In particular, the hard fact is that most fraud, within solicitors' firms, is committed at partner level.[8] The current version of the Solicitors' Accounts Rules is the best system it has been possible to devise which is of universal application, but that does not mean that they, and they alone, are the best system for any given firm. There is always room for improvements in systems, with checks and cross-checks that can be devised to fit a particular firm's requirements and circumstances. Whether or not these are a pervading theme throughout a firm's overall systematic management structure will be a test of its effectiveness.

Other compliance issues

Two specific compliance areas to be mentioned here are financial services and money laundering. It is not intended to go into any detail as to these matters. Suffice it to say that the Financial Services Authority's output of compliance requirements is of hitherto unprecedented length and complexity; and the laws on money laundering have undergone one major change and are about to undergo another.[9] What does need to be said, however, is that in assessing the overall effectiveness of a firm's systems, sufficient attention needs to be given to its capability to cope with these issues. This is particularly so because, ironically, the less a firm tends to deal with the areas in question, the more the danger may be, as the greater is the likelihood that staff will not be trained to spot, and will not be alert to, the danger signs. Thus awareness, training, and subsequent handling of problems in this area need to be carefully thought out in advance[10] and provided for in the systematic documentation available to all, such as the office manual.

The pay-off

The difficulty of establishing direct results

It was suggested above that insurance was just one of a number of risk control measures that a firm should adopt. In the same way, systematic management can be looked at as a form of insurance – the taking of steps which in 99 cases may not have any particular impact, in order to avoid the impact in the hundredth case. That being so, it is difficult to look for any quantifiable results, unless and until a claim is made. It has to be, to an extent, an act of faith.

The effect on professional indemnity insurance premiums

Paradoxically, the one area in which an effect is likely to be visible, and to a large extent quantifiable, is in regard to the level of the firm's indemnity insurance premium. Indeed, the promoters of some schemes, notably Lexcel, have been trying to persuade insurers to offer specific discounts to those with the appropriate certification. Insurers have however been reluctant to offer this direct linkage, not because they do not recognise the worth of Lexcel and its counterparts, but because they wish to assess the whole of a firm's risk profile, systems included, before quoting a price. In other words, if they were first to ignore a key part of that profile, quote an ostensible price, and then offer an arithmetical discount (e.g. '10 per cent off'), this would be merely a fictional means of including reference to the systematic part of the profile which the insurers would have considered anyway and to which they would, possibly, have attributed more importance than 10 per cent. It may therefore be that a standard saving cannot be defined. However, comparison with what the premium might have been under the old SIF regime, or indeed in a post-privatisation but pre-systematic era, will indicate the saving being achieved.

Indirect results

In any event, the indirect benefits of systematic management are likely to be as important as, if not more important than, the direct results. These benefits are manifold, but amongst the more important of them are likely to be:

- minimisation of uninsured risks;
- ensuring that staff are not overloaded, or asked to cope with areas in which they have no expertise, or left unsupported to manage files;
- a continual programme of improvement;
- a consistent standard of delivery of service; and
- higher levels of client satisfaction.

Future development within the profession

Improving client care may indeed be the key to the future development of such systems. The regime which in 2001 became established at the Law Society, after considerable debate within the profession, and under major pressure from the Lord Chancellor to put the profession's house in order or face that task being taken over by the government, is firmly and rightly centred on client care. That, in turn, means reliability and consistency of client care, which cannot in practice be achieved without systematic management. It may not be the case that Lexcel, or a similar system, becomes compulsory. Indeed, it is hoped that it should not, because those firms which have made the investment in a holistic system in order to obtain certification rightly feel that they should have a marketing edge over those who have not. The enthusiasm of those involved may vanish if the forces of compulsion fall upon them. It would be no surprise, however, to see those aspects of the Lexcel framework which most directly bear upon client satisfaction issues being incorporating into the Practice Rules as time goes on.

The new partner's perspective

What to look for

The underlying premise of this chapter is that a variety of factors require – and will increasingly require – a joined-up approach to the systems designed and operated by a firm. Thus the requirements of externally specified 'quality' management systems will be combined with appropriate risk control systems. The firm should also make the most of the opportunities offered by IT (without allowing IT suppliers to dictate systems or devoting an excess of resources to complying with IT requirements). The would-be partner should examine:

- the firm's existing systems, to see how well they fit those requirements;
- the willingness of the firm's management to espouse the concepts of systematic management generally;
- what resources are being devoted to the systems' actual operation and monitoring;
- the claims record of the firm, and in particular what trends it indicates, and how it may correlate with the implementation of systems which has already occurred;
- such evidence as there is of the direct results of what has already been achieved; and
- how systematic management is viewed as part of the firm's culture.

What the firm will be looking for

Any firm which already has systematic management principles in place will, when choosing a new partner, be likely to look at an individual's actual performance within those systems, and his willingness to expand his involvement with them. It will then consider what the record of claims and complaints may have been involving that individual. It will look at how he has performed at the routine tasks which form part of the system's requirements. Performance (if appropriate) in a supervisory role will be considered, as will any administrative tasks which may have been taken on. The prospective partner's general willingness to embrace change, and to accept the imperatives of a systematic approach, will be considered. For those firms which have further down the road to travel, the willingness of the individual to become involved in the process of system design may well be important. Essentially, any firm which sees its future as involving a substantial element of systematic management will be asking whether the potential new partner has a mindset which can adjust to, and make the best of, that way of working. The onus of proof will be on the applicant.

Notes

1   Klafter, C. and Walker, G. (1995) *Legal Practice Management and Quality Standards*. Blackstone Press.
2   This accords with the view expressed by Michael Power, to the effect that in many cases audits by quangos have become a deliberate and deceptive substitute for transparently government-based control, creating the illusion of supervision by independent bodies while maintaining the reality of centralised prescription: Power, M. (1999) *The Audit Society*, 2nd edn, Oxford University Press.
3   Source: Law Society December 2002.
4   See for instance Mayson, S. (1997) *Making Sense of Law Firms*, Blackstone Press, para 20.3, and Parasuraman, A., Zeithaml, V., and Berry. L. 'A conceptual model of service quality and its implications for future research', (1985) *Journal of Marketing*, Fall, p. 41.
5   Quite possibly in conjunction with the Law Society's Law Management Section.
6   Source: Bar Council website, January 2003.
7   There were, at the peak of the Assigned Risk's Pool's activities, 47 firms within it, according to the Law Society.
8   See Chapter 1, note 7.
9   With the coming into force of the Proceeds of Crime Act 2002, and the impending introduction into UK law of the requirements of the Second European Money Laundering Directive.
10 With such help as is available, e.g. the cards, guidance and CDs issued by or available from the Law Society in the case of money laundering.

Business development, strategy and planning

This chapter reviews the business planning requirements of a firm, and looks in some detail at the planning and analytical techniques which can be applied, to ensure all relevant factors are considered. A variety of ways in which each type of work can be evaluated are discussed. The processes of preparing a business plan are examined, as are the ways in which it can be adapted for its various audiences. Finally, it discusses the requirements for review of the plan, and the benefits of so doing.

The planning process in general

Introduction

Many different titles would have been suitable for this section, from strategy through planning to marketing. The common theme of all these areas is that they are designed to provide a focus on where the firm is going, and a process for analysing how best it can get there. Any prospective new partner who is contemplating committing himself to a firm for a major part of his professional life will want to know that the firm is already heading in a direction which he believes to be advantageous, and to be confident that he is equipped to play his part in shaping the future development of the organisation.

Assessing the firm's existing plans

It is unlikely that a new partner will, for some while at least, be able significantly to influence the strategic direction of the organisation, at least at firm-wide level. He may have more opportunity to do so at a departmental level, depending on the structure of the business. That is not to say, however, that he should not make himself aware of the existing plans, particularly insofar as they may affect him. Any of the quality assurance standards which may apply to the firm (e.g. Lexcel, Investors in People [IIP], the CLS Specialist Quality Mark, etc.) will include a requirement for the firm to have a business plan, which is formally reviewed at regular intervals, and against which the progress of the firm and departments is measured. Whether or not such standards are in place, the firm should have taken steps to ensure that all personnel, from senior partner to office cleaner, are aware, of the degree of detail that is appropriate to their position within the firm, of its strategic direction and ambitions. (This is an area upon which the IIP standard places particular emphasis.) If the firm is not clear in its direction, and partners have not disseminated sufficient information to staff for a prospective partner to make a preliminary assessment of the direction, then that of itself should be a cause for initial concern.

Considering the current business plan

The information distributed to staff may, however, be in fairly general terms. In order to get to grips with the underlying information, the prospective partner may need to ask the existing partners to show a copy of the plan to him. In some ways, this may prove to be as much a test of the firm's willingness to be open with the newcomer as a request for production of the accounts would be, for while the accounts are essentially historical, the business plan will be an exercise in prediction and, if it is to be complete, should have financial projections attached (see pp. 69–70 below).

The level at which the plan is considered

The overall plan for the firm will refer to several different levels if it is to be effective. At one end of the scale, it will be fairly general in its approach, setting out targets for total turnover or net profit per equity partner, and the sectors in which the firm will operate to achieve those targets. At the other end, it will descend to the level of operational planning and departmental work. These different aspects may be found in separate documents, or may be merged in one. The new partner may find it easier to relate to the departmental level targets for his own work area, since these will be much more closely allied to his own experience and knowledge. A review of this area may be the most appropriate place for him to formulate his own opinion on the practicality of the plan, although it would not necessarily be safe to extrapolate that view to the whole plan, i.e. just because the partners have formulated a workable plan for one department does not automatically mean that they have managed to do so across the firm. It is incumbent on the new partner to come to some conclusion on the thoroughness of the process applied generally, even if he does not feel that he is yet in a position to challenge the conclusions reached.

The intensity of planning

Another aspect to be considered is the degree to which the plan seems to be designed for the benefit of the firm, rather than for the greater satisfaction of the planner! It is very easy to become over-absorbed in the joys of the planning process for its own sake. Many firms will have been presented with a beautifully constructed plan, which has been approved and then totally ignored. Asking partners if they can actually lay their hands on the business plan for the firm is often a salutary experience!

Emergent strategies

It is important to make sufficient allowance within the plan for what Mintzberg[1] refers to as 'emergent strategy', i.e. ideas which 'can develop inadvertently, without the conscious intention of senior management, often through a process of learning'. Law firms are an ideal cradle for emergent concepts, for instance, where a lawyer becomes involved with an unusual case which achieves unexpected prominence and suddenly places him in the category of an 'expert' in that particular field, so that he is able to trade upon and develop that expertise into a new practice area.

Harmonising the concepts

What then should the new partner be looking for in assessing the firm's plan? Simply put, a mix of the two concepts of deliberate and emergent strategies. Deliberate and emergent strategies are not inimical to each other, but simply represent opposite ends of the spectrum which Mintzberg[2] identified, when he said: 'I believe that all viable strategies have emergent and deliberate qualities, since all must combine some degree of flexible learning with some degree of cerebral control.' His view of the desired process was that it should be '. . . capturing what the manager learns from all sources (both the soft insights from his or her personal experiences and the experiences of others throughout the organisation and the hard data from market research and the like) and then synthesizing that learning into a vision of the direction that the business should pursue'.

Establishing the firm's position

Placing the firm as it currently exists

For any plan, a starting point is needed. The first task is to establish where the firm is, in realistic terms, at the present time. Once the current status is known, it will be more feasible to make a practical assessment of the likelihood of moving towards the desired position. Mayson[3] posits 10 types of law firm, using the definitions set out below, and goes on to consider nine of those types (leaving aside the firm with international aspects). His classification can be represented as shown in Figure 4.1.

	Focused	Portfolio	General
Local			
Regional			
National			

Figure 4.1   Nine types of law firm, as posited by Mayson.
Source: Mayson, S. (2002) *Turning on to Strategy, Managing for Success,* Law Management Section, January. Reproduced by permission.

Terminology applicable to different types of firm

Some definition of the various terms is necessary, but this can be varied to suit the preferences of the analyst. Mayson suggests the following as a rough guide.

- Focused (a.k.a. 'niche') firms can expect to derive, say, over 50 per cent of turnover from one practice area, or 75 per cent from two areas.
- Portfolio firms can expect to derive more than 80 per cent of turnover from not more than four practice areas.
- General firms will cover most areas, but may still omit certain types of work.
- Local firms will be firmly rooted in their nearby geographical area, with one or more closely proximate offices.
- Regional firms will have more than one office, giving them geographical cover for an entire region, and allowing them to offer office-centred specialisations.
- National firms will cover the country, either in terms of their physical presence, or their client base, or both.

The terminology need not be too precise, for the purpose of the exercise is simply to consider what falls within a practical range of ambitions for the firm. For instance, a local portfolio firm might seek to become a regional portfolio firm, either by organic growth or by strategic merger, but it would not be realistic for it to expect to move rapidly towards a national presence. Mayson's structure is simply a framework, within which it is possible to test the viability of options which may emerge from other forms of analysis.

Assessing the influences on the firm

The next task is to examine the external factors which may influence the directions in which the firm moves. Lawyers being, in general, focused individuals, posing the question as to what pressures there may be upon the firm will normally evoke responses limited to their own narrow range of experience, i.e. what they perceive as direct threats to their own work area (by type or geographical location). They may not recognise the role played by external matters which are not legally specific, e.g. alterations in the prevailing macro-economic climate. What the planner needs to do, therefore, is to apply some predetermined method whereby data relating to all factors will be systematically input into the mix of information upon which the plan is based.

Available planning models

There are a large number of models, often represented in diagrams, which have been suggested. Though these of course differ, they all serve the same purpose, namely to help the planner to think logically through all aspects of the situation, and to marshal the information in a presentable and understandable manner.

Porter's 'Five Forces'

One of the most frequently encountered models is commonly known as 'Porter's Five Forces of Competition'. This was originally found in a seminal book by Porter,[4] but has been developed over the years by a number of others. One helpful variation is offered by Grant,[5] and is shown in Figure 4.2. Both the original and the adaptation attempt to group factors into five areas, and to represent the ways in which the pressures of four groups impact upon the fifth, central, group, namely competitive pressures within the industry in question. These four factors are pressures which may be exerted by:

- Suppliers of goods and services to the firm
- Clients and others buying services from the firm
- The ability of clients and others to buy services which, while different from those supplied by the firm, can be used as substitutes for them.
- Threats of others seeking to enter the industry in question, over and above existing competitors.

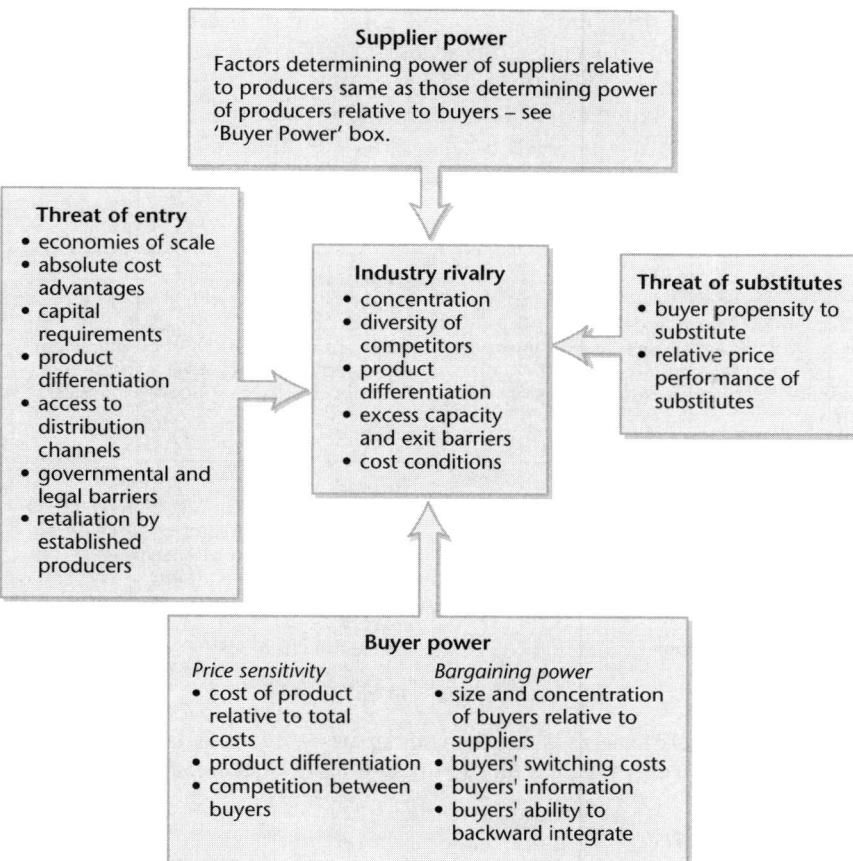

Figure 4.2   The determinants of competition and profitability within the Porter framework.
Source: Grant, R.M. (1995) *Contemporary Strategy Analysis*, Blackwell. Reproduced by permission.

SWOT analysis

A more simplistic, but similarly intentioned, technique is SWOT analysis. The four classifications of factors in this box form of analysis are:

- Strengths
- Weaknesses
- Opportunities
- Threats.

The drawback to this analysis is that it is less rigorous than Porter/Grant in forcing the planner to take into account all the external factors, the relevance of which may be less readily apparent, and it may therefore be more suited to detailed tactical decision-taking than to strategic thinking. It could, for instance, be used for assessing the methods whereby a firm could break into a new market area. An example showing this use of SWOT is shown in Figure 4.3.

Strengths	Weaknesses
Already do non-insolvency work for accountancy firms in question Expertise in similar areas, e.g. commercial contracts, litigation, etc. Profile in local professional community is high Reputation for efficiency is established	No senior solicitors with insolvency experience Competition with established practices supplying insolvency advice and services Lack of cashflow to support expansion
Opportunities	Threats
Expansion of business activity in insolvency due to recession Strengthening of position in overall commercial context Competition thought to be overpricing Counter-cyclical nature of work absorbing spare capacity	Fall-off of work when recession over Competition has greater resource base Adverse effect on relationships with non-insolvency accountants Cost affecting ability to expand existing areas of work Concentration of insolvency services by prospective clients in fewer (non-local) offices

Figure 4.3   SWOT analysis of establishing department to offer insolvency related services to major accountancy firms with insolvency departments.

Portfolio reviews

One of the exercises which should be conducted from time to time, and which may be done using the above tools or similar ones, is a review of the portfolio of services currently offered by the firm, and those it wishes to offer in future. For most firms, it will be possible to identify the portfolio as it exists fairly readily. Although firms may protest that they are ready, able, and willing to perform any task, none can actually cover all types of work. A non-exhaustive look at the types of work likely to be conducted by three typical firms may illustrate the breadth of the spectrum of work undertaken, as in Figure 4.4.

Linear development of services

In a simplistic way, Figure 4.4 also serves to illustrate the way in which service lines may develop or change. For instance:

- Few firms other than High Street ones now deal with criminal work, save for those which may make a specialty of, for instance, fraud.

High Street Firm	Large Provincial Firm	Major City Firm
Crime	Company / Commercial	Company / Commercial
Family (publicly funded)	Family (high value assets)	Mergers & Acquisitions
Conveyancing	Commercial Property	Banking/Asset Finance
Wills, Trust & Probate	Private Client	Private Client
Employment	Employment	Employment
Personal Injury	Civil Litigation	Commercial Litigation

Figure 4.4   Typical work carried out by different types of firm.

- Some services may translate across more than one type of firm, e.g. family law, but their approach is likely to develop, so that a High Street firm may take on all aspects of family work, including domestic violence, children, work, etc., but a mid-range firm may well have decided to concentrate on one particular area, e.g. dealing with ancillary relief cases involving high net worth families.
- Some services may trace across the entire spectrum, but again differ as they develop, so that with employment, for instance:
    - a High Street firm will act largely on the side of employees;
    - a provincial firm could act both for employees and employers from amongst its commercial client base; and
    - a City firm will only act on behalf of its institutional clients, advising on their generic employment practices.
- City firms will be the only firms with the reputation and resources to undertake certain types of work, such as mergers and acquisitions.

Of course, this analysis is over-simplistic, and the distinctions between the types of firm will always blur as one moves across the spectrum. However, it serves to illustrate the basic point, which is that what may appear to be the same type of services will develop and change as the firm changes, so the firm must analyse not only which services it wants to provide, but also what point of their development those services have reached.

Assessing different types of work

External forces

In considering each potential type of work (whether currently undertaken by the firm or not), there are a number of aspects which need to be considered. One question is what external forces are active or impact on the area under consideration. The nature of these forces will be varied, as illustrated by considering residential conveyancing, which could be affected by the factors in Figure 4.5. Any decision to include residential conveyancing in a portfolio, which did not take account of these factors, as well as the trends in those factors, would be incomplete.

External force	Example of effect
Macro-economic changes	A rise in interest rates affecting market conditions
Fiscal policy	A change in stamp duty provisions
Market perceptions	The concept of conveyancing becoming a 'shrink-wrapped' product for a fixed price, rather than a professional service
Market pressures	The potential impact of conveyancing call centres etc.
Regulatory relaxations	Opening the conveyancing arena to financial institutions
Demographic changes	The effect of an aging population in a particular area
Technological developments	The introduction of Land Registry-driven 'e-conveyancing'
Political pressures	The introduction of 'sellers' packs'

Figure 4.5   External forces in the area of residential conveyancing and their possible effects on the firm.

Human resources implications

A key to the analysis of any type of work is the availability of the resources necessary. Traditionally, these have largely been human resources, i.e. people with the skills to carry out the task. This element is of course still hugely important, and probably more difficult to address than before. In days gone by, most solicitors could be expected to be able to turn their hands to, if not everything which the firm did, then at least a reasonable range of work. Now, however, the training requirements of rapidly developing fields of law, and the dangers of practising in an area outside one's real expertise, have greatly increased the drive to specialisation. Further, there is now a greater need to ensure that the person handling a case has the appropriate level of qualification and experience. This is illustrated by the costs rules in civil litigation, which only allow the recovery of costs for the grade of fee earner which the court determines appropriate for the work, rather than allowing a solicitor to recover at the rate applicable to him. Not only specialisation, but also stratification within specialisations, is forced upon firms in many circumstances. Planners need to consider whether the firm truly has the right level of expertise (which may be subject to external assessment for certain types of work, such as those where Law Society Panels have been established) to be able to undertake a line of work safely and without risking both the reputation of the firm, and, through the negligence policies, the partners' pockets. If the firm has not, but wishes to take on such work, it will be necessary to consider whether it is feasible to acquire the expertise by straight recruitment, lateral hire, or by 'poaching' an entire department from another firm.

Technical resources

With any type of work, there is, of course, a need to provide some element of technical support.Word processing, computerised time recording and accounting packages are now taken for granted; increasingly, e-mail and internet facilities are falling into the same category. All of these serve to ramp up the capital investment required for the firm's operations generally. Certain areas, however, are now becoming much more capital intensive, as a result not only of internal requirements, but also external demands for technological advancement.

Using residential conveyancing as an example, many firms that wish to stay in this field will have concluded that they will require dedicated case management systems, with their attendant costs (i.e. not just acquisition and installation costs for the software but also training and maintenance). Now, if firms wish to be considered for bulk referral work from institutional introducers, they are likely to face demands that their systems must be adequate to provide information on the progress of the matter by electronic means (possibly e-mail but more likely web-based) to a range of third parties. Typically, these would be the client, the selling estate agent and (if different from the agent) the introducing institution. Each of those stakeholders may require different information. The costs of gearing up for such facilities, when matched against the commoditised price such bulk work brings, will force many firms to consider whether they are prepared to make the necessary investment. This process may well force a further instance of the linear development of services, as some firms will reject this option in favour of non-mechanised service which they believe they can sell at a higher price to their private client base, thus producing two distinct types of residential conveyancing work.

Profitability

An analysis of the profitability of each type of work will have to be undertaken. This is discussed in more detail in Chapter 7 in departmental terms. However, if a department crosses the boundaries of more than one type of work, it may be necessary, using the same techniques, to refine the analysis to examine separately the financial aspects of the different areas of work.

It is (subject to following paragraphs) axiomatic that the firm should not seek to do any line of work which is predicted to make a loss. A decision must be taken as to what represents the minimum level of profit. Inevitably, the rates will vary across the firm's service lines, and overall it is the average profit that will govern the return to partners. Equally, differentials between the profitability of areas of work will vary over time, e.g. with market trends. There should not, however, be too great a degree of cross-subsidisation, either in duration or relative percentage terms. Those whose work is subsidising that of others will become resentful, and it will become increasingly illogical to invest in lines which are not producing. Thus, the range of services that the firm offers should all yield anticipated profitability levels falling within a relatively tight range, and which will balance out over time.

Cashflow and funding implications

Firms also need to take account of two financial aspects which are not – at least at first sight – related to profitability. The first is the cashflow patterns of different types of work. For instance, while conveyancing is often thought of as being a low-profit area of work, it has the great advantage of being very positive in cashflow terms, in that clients can be asked to fund disbursements in advance, and most work will be billed and paid for as soon as it is completed, often within a few weeks of the work being started. Personal injury work, however, will often involve waiting years for payment, and acting as a client's banker in terms of the growing burden of disbursements for medical notes, consultants' reports, court fees, etc. The working capital requirements of undertaking only personal injury work would be severe, but a good conveyancing base can help to balance the problem. Further, property transactions tend to attract large sums of money into the client account, on which firms may still make good interest, within the relevant professional rules.

Non-financial elements

All of the above presupposes an entirely logical approach to the selection of services. However, logic is not always the only, or even the dominant, factor. Some firms will continue with relatively unprofitable lines of work because they believe that they are a service required by an identifiable block of clients from whom they attract other, more profitable, work: in effect, acting as a loss-leader. Others may try to be a 'full service' firm because they consider that the community they serve needs that range of services. Still others will act from pure altruistic principles, with financial reward being merely secondary. This may, for instance, apply to those practising in the human rights field. The writer recalls particularly one conversation with a criminal practitioner colleague who, when pressed as to why anyone in their right minds would wish to undertake criminal defence work, simply said: 'I know I'm a fool, but I passionately believe in it'. Society is lucky that there are still those with that attitude. The new partner will, however, probably want to ensure that a business plan which contains work undertaken for purely altruistic reasons also has some counter-balancing elements!

Risk elements

An additional field of analysis necessary, the importance of which has grown in recent years and continues to grow, is of the risks which attach to each type of work. The nature of risk which will occur most naturally to lawyers is professional negligence. Here, there is a wealth of available data on the inherent risks of different lines of work, from conveyancing at the most perilous end of the spectrum to employment, crime and immigration at the safest. Solicitors' Indemnity Fund annual reports give this information for previous years, and now that insurance is private, major insurance brokers report on the percentage of claims attracted by particular types of work (see the Law Society's *Gazette*). Negligence is, however, far from the only risk which should be considered. The likelihood of complaints being made and the resources necessary to handle them should be considered. A risk of a client defaulting on payment may be particularly associated with certain types of work, or there may be other financial risks attendant, such as 'no win, no fee' cases. Reputational risks may attach to certain areas, or even to particular high-profile and contentious clients.

Chapter 3 deals with systematic management requirements, and hence with risk issues, in more depth, but it is worth noting that Lexcel has led the way in this respect, and the CLS Specialist Quality Mark is following, with requirements that firms allocate risk ratings to each worktype, monitor performance against expectation at file level, collate the findings, and make whatever adjustments are indicated by the trends thus revealed.

Analysing the firm

Putting the pieces together

Analysing each potential area of work may involve a series of discrete exercises, perhaps involving different, if overlapping, groups of people. Simply adding together the results of those separate lines of enquiry may not, however, offer a cohesive business plan. Those factors which influence the firm as a whole also need to be considered. For instance, if the firm lies somewhere between the left-hand and middle columns in Figure 4.4 above, it will make little sense for some departments to press for a growth in commercial work, while others look for crime and welfare work. All this would achieve would be a divided firm. The unit as a whole needs to move in the same direction, and that may entail sacrificing some plans which, viewed on a stand-alone basis, might seem desirable.

Taking a financial overview

When assembling the overall plan, it is equally necessary to take account of the overall financial position of the firm. There may have to be a choice between two promising lines of work, if there is only sufficient finance available to invest in one. In this situation, the financial consequences of each alternative, in terms of return on capital invested, profitability, cash-flow, etc., and any non-financial aspects (e.g. any tie-in with existing client groups) will need to be tested against each other. Equally, the potential risks of different types of work will need to be examined, so that, for instance, a firm does not commit all its available investment potential to areas such as 'no win, no fee' cases which may lead to expenditure being incurred without return.

Preparing the plan

The personal consequences of choice

A partner who is new to the process of business planning may, at this stage, be somewhat surprised at how passionate discussions may become! Choices between different areas of work may have consequences which will affect partners personally, and the selection may not be easy or unanimous. Partners in charge of departments which are the beneficiaries of investment may forget that their success was achieved at the price of the ambitions of partners who wanted to focus elsewhere, and the latter may become resentful. These feelings may spread over into departmental staff. It is important for all partners to keep in mind that the planning process is for the long-term benefit of all, and to disseminate that view throughout the firm.

Ensuring current and realistic challenges

As will be shown below, any plan needs to have quantified goals. Another key to coordinating the final plan is to assess the degree of challenge which the plan sets for all concerned. Although the plan should be achievable, it should not be too easy. Some firms have been known to come up with plans which essentially say: 'We'll keep doing what we have been, but just do it a bit better.' Such plans pose no challenge at all, and will be demotivating for the firm's personnel. Equally, if a plan sets too high a target, e.g. promising 50 per cent growth in turnover within a year, then staff will regard it as unrealistic, and simply ignore it.

Focusing the objectives

Many business plans will operate at two levels. On the one hand, they will be aspirational, making general statements about the ambitions of the firm. On the other, they will be specific about the steps to be taken, and the goals to be set. Aspirational statements cannot stand alone as a plan. No plan will be successful as a tool unless it is expressed in terms which the people responsible for implementation can relate to their performance, both in terms of what is to be achieved and what has already been done.

The usual acronym is that the plan should be expressed in terms which are 'SMART', i.e.:

- Specific – as mentioned above, vague statements may be acceptable as precursors to a plan, but will have no part to play in the statement of actual goals.
- Measurable – where at all possible, goals should be stated in terms which can be measured objectively, e.g. a percentage rise of x per cent. If some aims seem difficult to express in these terms, it will be necessary to create other ways of measuring them. For instance, if raising the firm's profile is a serious goal, it might be appropriate to commission market research at the beginning and end of the plan's life to assess its impact; otherwise the success or failure of any efforts made will be assessed solely by the partners' subjective views.
- Agreed – there is no point in setting targets to which people will pay only lip service, because they do not really accept them. Some writers speak of people 'buying into' or 'owning' goals.
- Realistic – if a goal is over or under ambitious, it will be demotivating or simply ignored.
- Timed – it is essential that a time is set for the attainment of any goal set. Otherwise, the goal will descend from the practical to the aspirational. Like all other aspects, the time limit should be realistic but challenging.

Allocating responsibilities

Having set out the aims which the firm seeks to achieve, the time frame within which they are to be attained, and the means by which they are to be measured, the plan must go on to consider how all of that is to be done. First and foremost, it needs to set out whose responsibility it is to see that necessary steps are taken. Unless someone is plainly accountable, little will happen. Those responsible have to accept that their performance is a matter of importance to them and others. In firms which operate performance-based reward systems (see Chapter 9) this is likely to be reflected in their remuneration.

Allocating resources

The next step is a collective one, in that the plan needs to indicate what resources will be allocated to the person responsible to enable that person to implement any change. This may be the people to be assigned or hired to work in the department; the marketing budget to be allocated; or the capital investment in the necessary IT infrastructure. In other words, having allocated someone the job, the plan must give that person the tools to do it.

Managing the change

All plans will involve some degree of change. Some changes will simply be incremental. Some, however, may be dramatic, e.g. closing an unprofitable department on the one hand, or investing heavily in IT systems and recruiting extra for a department to be enlarged on the other. The plan should therefore consider what steps may need to be taken to manage the change. The plan should consider whether the person responsible for implementing the change will need help and/or resources specifically directed to controlling the process which is inherent in reaching the target set. This might, for instance, take the form of external counselling for staff, or the hiring of external trainers; or it might be as simple as an allowance against normal targets for the time which must be invested in order to achieve a smooth transition.

Consultation when preparing the plan

We have looked at the functions a business plan needs to fulfil and its main features. However, the way in which it should be put together, i.e. the process of compiling it, has not yet been considered. This will obviously vary greatly from firm to firm, but some common themes can be identified. To start, someone must be allocated the responsibility to ensure it happens. This may be an individual or a team. It should not be the case, however, that those responsible are the only people involved in the plan's preparation. They should consult as widely as they feel will be feasible. This may be through their direct involvement, or by delegating parts of the process down the pyramid of the firm's management structure.

The consultation needs to be carefully handled, in order to keep a forward-looking focus, but subject to that caveat it can be a creative process in two ways. First, it will mean that those who eventually put the plan together have information as to what the real situation is, as perceived by those at operational level, and not what they, the planners, think it ought to be. Second, it will make all those consulted feel a part of an inclusive process, so that when the plan emerges they do not feel it has been imposed on them from above. (The corollary is that it is necessary to avoid raising expectations unrealistically during the consultation process, e.g. by promising resources which, as it turns out later, cannot be provided.)

Considering infrastructure elements

The consultation process must extend to consideration of all infrastructure elements, and those who are involved in organising those elements of the firm's operation. In smaller firms, that may of course be the partners themselves, but in larger ones it will include those with responsibility for a variety of functions, e.g.:

- Marketing – how easy will it be to sell the services which the plan resolves upon, and what measures will be necessary?
- Human resources – will the firm have the range of competencies and expertise, and the support staff, required to implement the plan?
- IT – what technology will be involved in delivering the services?
- Finance – see below.

Considering financial elements

Many firms at the less sophisticated end of the spectrum will only recently have progressed from the stage where their business planning consisted of merely formulating an annual budget. No matter how complex the planning process may become, it should not be forgotten that financial considerations lie at the heart of it. Those responsible for the firm's financial management must be involved at all stages, and a plan is likely to contain the means by which future success or failure will be judged. These may, for instance, include the following:

- *Profit and loss account.* This is an essential part of the exercise, since it will show the intended effect of the plan on the profitability of the firm, and highlight flaws. For instance, it may show that the planned expansion will increase turnover considerably, but at a slower rate than the increased expenditure needed to generate that turnover, so that the net profit per partner could be expected to decrease. Subsidiary accounts on a departmental basis may be needed as well.
- *Cashflow projection.* Profit is a paper concept, and cash is a real one. The plan needs to indicate what the cash movements would be. Take a situation where growth in turnover entailed up-front

investment, but was in a field which meant slow progress from incurring expenditure to payment of bills. An example might be the cost of installing a case management system for litigation on behalf of a client that was unwilling to accept interim billing. The potentially dangerous cashflow consequences of this upon the firm's working capital requirements would be shown by the cashflow projections.

- *Balance sheet projections.* These may be less frequently found, but they flow from the cashflow and profit and loss projections so are not unduly difficult to construct; they are particularly useful if the firm is, for instance, seeking external financing based on the plan's projections.
- *Sensitivity analysis.* This is a relatively sophisticated tool which demonstrates the effects of deviation from the estimates made in projections. Thus, the profit and loss account might be based on a growth of 15 per cent in turnover, which would be reflected in the cashflow projection. What, however, would be the effect if the 15 per cent turned out actually to be 5 per cent? Would a positive cashflow trend turn into a negative one? This analysis would help to illustrate how risky the plan is in financial terms.

The time frame

The longer the time frame of any plan, the less accurate any projections are likely to be. Predicting, for instance, the effect of changes in the macro-economic climate in which the firm operates is difficult enough over one year, but virtually impossible over five years. Most plans, therefore, will inevitably be more aspirational, and involve more in the way of estimation, over the later years. Firms will need to judge for themselves the length of time for which they wish construct plans (this may be dictated by the requirements of others, e.g. finance sources). Specific goals, which fulfil the SMART criteria referred to above, are likely to be restricted to the early life of the plan.

Determining the plan's readership

When it comes to putting the plan on paper, those responsible will have the choice of a wide range of styles, all of which may be appropriate to particular circumstances. Some may be little more than a series of bullet points, with financial consequences attached. Some may take the form of a flow diagram, with each objective broken down into sub-objectives and so on. Others may be textual, and even fairly discursive, provided that the necessary detail is clearly included as well.

Deciding on the style to be adopted will involve determining the audience that the plan is intended to reach. First and foremost, the plan should be designed for use by the partners themselves as a working tool. Firms will also want to use the plan as a means of communicating the firm's current position and future plans to its staff (even if some financial elements are omitted from this version) and indeed this may be required by some quality assurance standards as a way of demonstrating the staff's knowledge of the firm's development. The plan may be required by those who provide financial support to the firm, who need to know more than the historical information that the firm's accounts reveal. Others may wish to use the plan, or elements of it, as part of their marketing drive to existing and prospective clients. For example, they may need to demonstrate to a client that their tender of services is part of a carefully determined strategy which they have the resources to deliver, and not an over-optimistic attempt to punch above their real weight.

Communicating, reviewing and changing the plan

Précising the plan and issuing mission statements

As mentioned, it may be appropriate for different audiences to receive different versions or different parts of the plan. The firm may want to abridge the plan for general distribution. The ultimate form of this process of reduction is the publication of a 'mission statement', i.e. a pithy sentence or two that encapsulate the firm's raison d'être. Opinions differ on mission statements. They may be an inspirational tool, or they may be so vague as to be mere 'marketing-speak'. Firms operating in heterogeneous markets over a variety of fields will find it particularly difficult to differentiate themselves in this way, and hence will be forced towards blandness. Those which have niche practices, or demonstrate unusual cultural aspects, may find it easier and more productive to formulate mission statements in a concise and informative manner.

Reviewing the plan

Most of the quality assurance standards require that the plan is regularly and formally reviewed by the partners at, e.g. annual or six-monthly intervals. Sadly, some firms view this as meaningless bureaucratic necessity, and believe they have done enough if the partnership minutes can state: 'The business plan was reviewed.' Such firms might as well scrap the plan (if indeed they can find it in the first place). Any new partner who finds that this is his firm's attitude will have real cause for concern. This attitude means that no-one is ever accountable for delivering on the projections and promises made. Rather, the review of the plan should be used as an opportunity to:

- See how plans are progressing against the measures set for their success, e.g. if 15 per cent growth was forecast for a year, how much has been achieved in the first six months, and if delivery is not on target what steps are needed to put the plan back on course?
- Test the assumptions which underlay the plan, e.g. if financial projections were based on paying a certain interest rate on working capital, what effect have market forces actually had, and what are the consequences of this?
- Assess the actual input of resources against what was projected.
- Consider the impact of any unforeseen circumstances.

Changing the plan

No plan is ever going to reflect reality with 100 per cent accuracy. A review may indicate that the divergences from the plan are relatively minor, and within acceptable tolerances, so there is no need for any major changes. It may, however, show that there are major problems, which result not from a defect in the original plan, but from unavoidable external circumstances. If no changes are made, and hence the targets set for those affected are not altered, it may become demoralising for the individuals affected to realise both that they are falling behind expectations, and that there is little that they can do to improve the situation. In such circumstances, it is advisable to make a formal interim alteration to the plan. An active and realistic review process will also make the task of formulating the next fully-worked plan much easier, since the base from which the planners will be starting will more closely resemble reality.

Notes

1   Mintzberg, H.: 'The Fall and Rise of Strategic Planning' (1994) *Harvard Business Review*, Jan/Feb, p. 107.
2   Ibid.
3   Mayson, S. 'Turning on to Strategy' (2002) *Managing for Success, Law Management Section*, January.
4   Porter, M. (1980) '*Competitive Strategy: Techniques for Analysing Industries and Competitors*', Free Press.
5   Grant, R.M. (1995) '*Contemporary Strategy Analysis*', Blackwell.

5

Marketing techniques

This chapter offers a variety of ways in which a new partner may approach the problem of developing his client base, and fulfilling his part of the firm's business plan. It looks first at issues relating to the knowledge of clients and their needs, and the methods by which client retention and the acquisition of new clients can be improved. It then goes on to consider various ways of communicating the firm's message to existing and prospective clients, through both profile-raising and specific advertising, including such tools as brochures and websites. The possibilities of TV and radio advertising are reviewed, and the issues raised by externally driven marketing and introduction schemes are examined.

General

Introduction

This chapter has very deliberately been headed 'marketing techniques' rather than simply 'marketing', since the concept of marketing, i.e. differentiating the firm's services and selecting the services to be offered, has been dealt with in the previous chapter. This chapter looks at the ways in which the firm may seek to achieve, in hard, practical, terms, the goals that it has set itself in terms of client acquisition, client retention, and penetration into particular markets. From the new partner's perspective, this chapter is essentially a toolbox, containing a number of mechanisms with which he will be expected to become familiar himself, and from which he can pick when it comes to fulfilling his own entrepreneurial goals in terms of the performance of his own department, or the firm generally.

The relationship between marketing and selling

The terms 'marketing' and 'selling' may at first sight seem synonymous, but in fact the former is much broader than the latter. 'Selling', in terms of turning a nascent solicitor–client relationship into concrete instructions, is of course a vital part of marketing, but there is much marketing work to be done, in most cases, before that final stage approaches.

The more successful the marketing labours, the less arduous will be that last push. Some firms now require new partners (perhaps even as part of the partner selection process) to formulate their own personal business plans, identifying areas where they will be seeking growth for themselves and their team, and how they intend to achieve that growth. Plans need to cover all stages of marketing, not only up to the point where services are sold, but also beyond this to the ways in which first instructions will be turned into repeat business. This chapter is intended to assist new partners in both the formulation and the execution of these plans.

Client knowledge, retention and acquisition

Client knowledge

The first step is getting to know the client base. That may seem obvious, because the new partner is likely to have acquired during his previous years with the firm (unless laterally hired into the partnership position) a knowledge of the clients with whom he has come into contact. It may well be, however, that the partner has never analysed what sector(s) of the community, whether private or commercial, makes up the backbone of his department's or the firm's client base. That may particularly be true for a new partner who has previously worked within a department of narrow scope, with clients drawn from a relatively narrow selection of commercial or institutional organisations, and who now has to think on a firm-wide basis for the first time.

Identifying gaps in the client base

One aspect of the client base the new partner should consider is not what the client base is, but rather what it is not. In other words, are there potential areas which the firm does not currently reach? If, for instance, the firm acts for a group of insurers in motor accident claims, does it also act for those insurers' property insurance claims departments? Or, if the firm has a solid commercial base, is it also doing the private work of all those managers and directors with whom it comes into contact? This analysis may well open up areas for possible cross-selling, which is discussed in more detail below.

Relating the client base to services offered

Another aspect of the client base which can usefully be considered is how well it sits with any new services that the firm has decided to offer. If, for example, the firm has decided to target net high worth individuals for wills and retirement planning services, does the firm's existing client profile offer a reasonable chance of reaching that market sector? Which of the marketing techniques outlined below may be the most suitable for the task of changing that profile to a material extent?

Use of client databases

Amongst the most frequently available, and in practice one of the least successfully used, aspects of information technology is the client database. For several years, many firms will have had available to them database facilities, giving not just a central record of clients' names and addresses, but scope for analysing this information by age, location, wealth brackets, commercial interests, personal interests, etc. Far too many such databases lie fallow, however, and even the most basic of information either is not completed or is allowed to become outdated. A classic example is failing to update clients' addresses even though the conveyancing department has carried out the sale and purchase work for the move! The legal profession is not alone in this – the correspondence columns of the broadsheets often contain indignant examples of the ludicrous mistitled and missent correspondence to which over-reliance on an unchecked computer database may give rise. The problem is that a database which is not accurate may be worse than useless. It may even be positively dangerous to the reputation of the firm, e.g. by incurring the opprobrium of a widow to whose deceased husband the firm has just written. The new partner should therefore take steps to find out how reliable and useful the database actually is, and should note what steps need to be taken for improving it, e.g. by clarifying lines of control and responsibility for its updating.

Ascertaining the client's views of the firm

The new partner should also acquaint himself with the results of any market research undertaken to find out what the client base thinks of the firm. The results can often be surprising, and will help to indicate how successful the firm is in its efforts to become client focused, in terms of providing the service and outcome which clients actually want, as distinct from what firms think they want. Many surveys have shown the two sets of criteria to be widely different![1]

Client questionnaires

An increasing number of firms ask clients to complete a questionnaire to indicate their views of the firm. These may be sent on a random sample basis, or even to each client on the termination of a retainer. Care needs to be used to draw a balance between, on the one hand, sending out sufficient numbers to get a statistically valid sample response, and, on the other, avoiding over-burdening clients who give repeat instructions by sending them a questionnaire in respect of every single job. Considerable thought also needs to be given to the design of the questionnaire in order to identify criteria which are of real significance to the client. This means that issues such as responsiveness and accessibility should be addressed, as much as whether the case was won or lost. Vital information on potential areas for improvement can be derived from such an exercise. New partners who find that their departments have never carried out such an exercise should instigate one.

Client interviews and surveys

A linked concept is that of carrying out more detailed examinations of client perceptions by means of client interviews and/or surveys. These can be carried out by members of the firm itself. Opinions differ as to whether this exercise is better done by client-facing personnel, e.g. the partner with whom a client may deal, or by those divorced from case-handling, such as a marketing manager. Alternatively, and particularly in the case of formal surveys, they can be carried out by independent consultants or market research agencies. The advantage in using people other than case handlers, whether from within the firm or outside it, is simply that some clients may give their true views more freely when dealing with someone new. It is, after all, no use to be told simply what the respondent to a survey may think you want him to say. There are obviously costs associated with this work, both in direct terms and in the opportunity costs associated with setting up and analysing the results of the exercise. However, those who have taken this option acknowledge the benefit of the outcome – even if they have not liked what they have been told. For their part, clients are normally pleased to be consulted, and fewer than expected will claim that they are too busy to participate. Some will be flattered that their views are considered to be of sufficient importance for them to be consulted.

What do non-clients think?

An obvious drawback with the concept of questionnaires or surveys of clients is that they are by definition self-selecting. They draw upon the opinions of those who have already been sufficiently affected by the firm's previous marketing efforts to have given instructions to that firm in the first place. Unless things are radically wrong, a significant proportion of these clients should be expected to be at least broadly satisfied, or repeat instructions would simply dry up. What though of all those who have not chosen to instruct the firm? Why not? It may therefore be desirable to find out what those who are not clients may think. If, for instance, your firm acts for 10 of 30 institutions in a discrete commercial sector, it might be useful to conduct a survey of the other 20, to discover generally what criteria they use to select their lawyers and/or specifically why they may have chosen not to instruct your firm. Few firms undertake this sort of project, yet they might benefit from it, particularly if seeking to expand market share in an existing line of service.

Client recovery

Any technique designed to ascertain what is important to clients will come into its own when the concept of client retention is considered. It is axiomatic that it is easier to sell services to existing clients than to new ones. How then has the firm performed in terms of retaining its clients? Are there any common themes to the reasons why clients may choose not to reinstruct the firm? What useful information is on the database? For instance, it may be possible to show that a particular partner, or department, loses a greater proportion of clients than others. It will be less easy to find out that the reason that clients are leaving is that the receptionist is rude to them, or the fee earners communicate in terms which are considered patronising. Some effort at exit interviews, similar to those conducted with departing staff, may be beneficial if former clients are known to be placing their instructions elsewhere. Even if the information only helps to avoid losing other clients, the endeavour will be worthwhile, giving the former client the opportunity to voice, possibly for the first time, any frustrations with the service received, which may subsequently be overcome for this or other clients.

Client retention

Client retention is a subject all of its own. It pays to remember that, at its core will be the personal relationship between the fee earner(s) involved and the individual(s) who are the client (even if acting in their capacity as managers of an institutional client). Of course, in some cases, clients' decisions about buying services may be driven entirely by price or, at institutional level, be subject to the edicts of higher authorities who never, in practice, interact with their suppliers of legal services.

The fact remains that, if all other factors are equal, any individual will prefer to deal with someone with whom he has a good relationship. Those personal relationships are not always a matter of chance – they will often need to be carefully considered and worked on – but they are central to any firm's success in retaining its client base. One aspect of this is the need to control the situation which occurs when one end of that chain breaks down, e.g. the departure of the fee earner in question. It is at that stage that the firm's ability to institutionalise the knowledge base of its fee earners, e.g. by recording the individual likes and dislikes of particular clients, and their preferred methods of working, will come to the fore.

Maintaining the client relationship

Many of the techniques which are relevant to client retention will, of course, be just as pertinent to the recruitment of new clients, but it is important to remember that they must also be deployed in respect of existing clients. It is all too easy to concentrate on the excitement of attracting potential new 'targets' at the expense of nurturing existing ones. (New partners should, in this connection, note whether, in measuring, and perhaps rewarding, their performance, the firm's systems recognise successful retention as much as adding new clients – see Chapter 8.) When considering the factors important for client retention, lawyers almost invariably give too much prominence to technical legal ability. In the great majority of cases, this is a factor which only comes into play in a negative sense. Thus, clients will of course react adversely if something goes wrong, but otherwise they will take it as a given that someone practising in the relevant work area has the technical competence to do so. There will of course be exceptions to this, where an extra degree of expertise or specialism is required. But in most cases, simply carrying out the task competently will not be enough.

Retention techniques

What many clients are looking for are facets of service that will, to use with due apology an overworked phrase, 'add value' to the basic constituents of the service to be provided. Tools at the firm's disposal, all of which are dealt with in more detail below, include:

- hospitality at sporting or cultural events;
- gifts at Christmas or other suitable occasions;
- the straightforward, and not-yet-dead, business lunch;
- invitations to general seminars, etc.;
- in-house seminars or presentations exclusively for the client's staff;
- newsletters;
- updates on legal developments affecting specific client groups;
- staff exchanges or secondments; and
- discounted service facilities for a client's staff.

Care needs to be taken when providing hospitality, gifts, etc. to be sensitive to restrictions on the part of the recipient, especially for those in public service.

Tendering to existing clients

A growing feature of life in the provision of commercial legal services to bulk buyers is the tender, not just for new work or to new clients, but also to existing clients. A good example is the insurance industry, where a combination of a shrinking number of increasingly globalised insurers and growing pressure for cost and efficiency improvements has led to a remorseless process of reduction in the size of the panels of firms which are maintained. Sometimes, the other tenderers will be firms that are also already doing that company's work (albeit in other places), but sometimes new firms are added to the mix. Often, the 'carrot' to persuade a firm to improve its offering is that, if successful, it will receive a bigger share of the company's work. Much of what is required will be the same as for other tenders, but at least the firm has the chance to use its knowledge of the client's needs and views and to play to its strengths in formulating its tender proposals. Yet again, the importance of an awareness of the client's perceptions of the services offered by the firm emerges.

Knowledge of new clients

It is not only in respect of the retention of existing clients, however, that knowledge will count. Researching prospective clients is just as important in winning new business. For instance, a new partner who, in his spare time, has established a reputation and contacts in a particular field, e.g. volunteering with a charitable organisation, may realise that he has the core of a potential client grouping for advice on charity law. Research may, however, be much more sophisticated, and may cover a wide range up to the employment of market research agencies to investigate a particular target market group, or even an individual target organisation, e.g. where a tendering opportunity is presented. All too often, lawyers have been too reactive in such circumstances, and have not devoted the same effort and resources to finding out about their prospects as would routinely be deployed by marketing departments in the commercial world.

Specific marketing initiatives

Advertising in general

In essence, most marketing techniques are about imparting to a target audience as much relevant information about the firm as is needed to persuade them to instruct the firm. Often, that information may be planted a long time before any results are seen. Nowhere is this more likely to be the case than in the instance of straightforward advertising, particularly advertising that is aimed at general profile raising, rather than at a particular service or client group. Consequently, the value of advertising, in terms of direct results and return on investment is notoriously difficult to assess. In many instances it is an act of faith. In the legal profession, many of whose senior members still remember with clarity and perhaps fondness the times when advertising of any sort was a serious breach of professional rules, there is often a lack of enthusiasm for advertising. The result is that the quality of advertising is poor, and fails to convey to the public any sense of what makes that particular firm special.

Advertising in the context of a professional firm

That old sense that advertising is somehow demeaning for a proper profession has lingered on for longer than might have been expected. Until very recently, for example, although mailshotting the public was permitted, the Solicitors' Publicity Code dictated that mailings could not be followed up by a telephone call to recipients – a basic tenet of successful marketing of this sort. Even now, the relaxation of the rules applies only to prospective business and commercial clients, not private clients. Further, there is still the feeling that some types of advertising are inappropriate for professional firms, e.g. the seemingly ambulance-chasing television campaigns in the claimant personal injury world from the 'claims farmer' companies which have advertised so successfully; or the notorious (but apparently rewarding) 'Ditch the Bitch' campaign for family work conducted by one firm. The approach taken to advertising should be suitable for the developing culture of the firm.

Branding by advertising

A certain level of profile-raising advertising is likely to be used by most firms. It will vary greatly in form, from an advert within a programme for a local sporting or charitable event, through the production of a brochure, to the general information pages of a website. The message should be simple, clear, and presented in a consistent and professional manner which is instantly recognisable by the logo, form of presentation, or 'house style' used. As a part of the process of 'branding' the firm, profile advertising has an important – but long term – part to play. All media exposure and advertising for the firm should follow the brand.

Specific advertising campaigns

The same branding techniques should also run through any specific advertising campaigns. There are additional criteria which can be applied here to monitor the success and value of campaigns. A campaign targeted at a specific service the firm provides and/or at a particular client group, offers a much better chance of ascertaining the response rate. This could be done simply by asking new clients why they have given instructions to the firm, or by monitoring the number of new instructions received in the relevant area during or soon after the period of the campaign. The key point is to be able to ascertain from the clients' communications that they come as a result of the advertising. Other devices such as reply-paid cards, specific e-mail addresses, dedicated telephone lines, etc. all allow the firm to see clearly what response has been generated by their investment. Only then will the managers of the firm really know whether the campaign is worth repeating.

Brochures

Brochures are a sub-species of advertising which allows the communication of information to prospective clients about the firm, its personnel, its aims and culture, and the services it offers. For many firms, however, brochures have been little but an expensive waste of resources. Anecdotal evidence abounds of firms which spent many hours of partners' time arguing about the content, layout and cost of brochures which ended up in piles scattered around offices for years, unloved and undistributed! It is crucial to have a clear concept from the start of what a particular brochure is intended to do, and how it is to do it, i.e. what message is it to convey, to what audience, and by what means it is to be distributed to that audience. Used with that degree of clarity, a brochure becomes a powerful means of communication, and a chance to enhance a firm's image. If a series of brochures or leaflets is to be used, the 'house style' should be consistently applied and clearly evident.

Letterheads, etc.

It may seem strange to refer to letterheading (and similar materials such as invoices, business cards, etc.) in a chapter on marketing, but again they are simply aspects of the firm's presentation of itself to the outside world. The issue of 'house style' applies here, as do the needs for clarity and the choice of the method of presentation of information. The need for a straightforward layout is becoming increasingly important as the amount of data on letterheads increases, with direct telephone and fax numbers, direct e-mail addresses, quality assurance and specialist panel accreditations, etc. being included. Badly managed, this information can become so intrusive that it becomes difficult to use the first page of the letter. Designers need to consider what information is important, and where it can most easily be accessed.

Websites

General

The use of websites is almost a separate subject of its own. Like the early days of brochures, many mistakes have been made, and many partners have been disappointed that their brand new, and possibly highly expensive, website has not suddenly produced a massive influx of new instructions. Again, it is a question of understanding the purpose of any particular site. At its most basic, a site will act as a general brochure, i.e. containing general (and, in many cases, fairly anodyne and uninteresting) information about the firm. Further, a website is potentially less valuable than a brochure, since the firm can decide to whom brochures are to be distributed; a website, however, depends upon prospective readers taking proactive steps to access it. There is nothing wrong with a website conveying general information, so long as the limitations of this are recognised, and it is taken as the start of the process of site development, and not an end in itself.

Direct marketing using the internet

It is beyond the scope of this work to deal in any detail with the myriad ways by which websites *can* work very successfully as direct marketing exercises. However, it is important to recognise at the outset the resources which will be needed to get such a site up and running, and (just as importantly) to maintain it. This applies whether it is a relatively simple concept such as the automatic production of a document like a will in response to a sequence of questions, or the ambitious creation of a massive store of specialist (and hence highly valuable) information such as the 'Blue Flag' financial services industry site created by (as it then was) Linklaters.

Some 'don'ts' for websites

There are also some instances where websites can be a significantly negative factor. Examples are:

- Wasting resources by putting vast amounts of free information and advice on sites, without ever thinking how this effort is to be converted into instructions or money.
- Designing sites so that they frustrate the user by requiring them to wait while large images or flash animations are loaded.
- Leaving rapidly aging information on ostensibly 'news' oriented sites.
- Failure to meet the expectation of rapid response invariably generated by inviting clients to communicate electronically.

Television and radio advertising

Comparatively few law firms have commissioned TV advertising. Partly this has been because of the sensitivities around 'professional' status mentioned above, but more importantly it has been the result of the prohibitive cost of first making, and secondly broadcasting, suitable commercials. A greater number of firms have tried radio campaigns with local broadcasters, where cost is reduced. Recently however, the power of TV advertising, when linked to the consumer demand for legal services, has been amply demonstrated by the rash of personal injury claims-handling firms who have founded businesses on the strength of their TV campaigns.[2] In some instances, these have been copied either by individual firms, or by consortia formed to take advantage of the regional spread of TV companies' broadcasts, and share the costs accordingly with, for instance, centralised (and possibly outsourced) call handling facilities, and the division of enquiries by geographical location of the enquirer, and/or by rota. Radio or TV campaigns have frequently been single issue projects, meaning that the return on investment could be relatively easily monitored. Also, the motto of 'little and often' has been a guiding principle, with frequency of broadcast being of high importance. It remains to be seen whether firms/consortia will be sufficiently pleased with the results of their efforts to broaden the scope of their advertising. If so, this may prove to be a motivation to mould more formal regional alliances or even mergers, to take advantage of the regional presence which might thus be capable of being established.

Marketing groups

There are a number of more or less formalised marketing groups within the profession who have conducted joint media campaigns at various levels. Generally these groups have something more in common than a mere desire to begin an advertising campaign, e.g. they already exist as groups for management consultancy and training purposes, or they all adhere to a minimum level of quality assurance, etc. The difficulty with such joint efforts is the necessity of attracting enough commitment in a sufficiently short period of time to achieve the economies of scale which will make the exercise truly effective. A strong centralised drive is required for success.

Payment of 'marketing fees'

In recent years, a number of schemes have flourished whereby firms 'buy' work from institutional introducers, largely in the consumer-oriented areas of personal injury and conveyancing, by agreeing to pay contributions to the cost of the introducers' own marketing campaigns, often calculated by reference to the number of referrals they receive. Thus the profession's inability to resource or coordinate its own advertising campaigns has resulted in the situation where others, such as claims-handling firms, legal expenses insurers and chains of estate agents, who are willing and able to commit themselves to advertising campaigns, have the cost of those campaigns subsidised by the lawyers who actually do the work anyway! The fragility of some of these schemes has been reflected in the much-publicised business failures of some of the introducers,[2] which in turn have threatened and caused damage to many solicitors' firms who were participating in the schemes. Further, their legality under the Solicitors' Introduction and Referral Code is often dubious, and in at least one instance the court has declared them to be against the Code,[3] with the consequence that fees paid by firms operating the offending scheme were claimable neither from the losing insurer nor the client on whose behalf they had ostensibly been paid. Efforts to abolish or relax the Code have to date been unsuccessful, and some clarification may be expected in advance of an increase in efforts to enforce its provisions.

Future developments recording 'marketing fees'

New partners would do well to consider, therefore, the extent to which their firms may have become reliant on such practices, and hence vulnerable to requests for increases in contributions and where rapid increases in costs can readily make the difference between the work being profitable or not. New partners should also consider whether the decision-making processes within their firms are capable of improvement, and whether the resources available can be increased, in order for their own advertising campaigns to become viable without the need for such external dependency. This is one area where, if the professional rules which restrict the obtaining of equity capital from non-solicitor investors are relaxed, as approved in principle by the Law Society in March 2002, the opportunity for access to resources presently undreamed of could well be utilised.

Notes

1   See for instance Mayson, S. (1997) *Making Sense of Law Firms*, Blackstone Press, para 20.3, and Parasuraman, A., Zeithaml, V. and Berry, L. 'A conceptual model of service quality and its implications for future research' (1985) *Journal of Marketing*, Fall, p. 41.

2   E.g. Claims Direct.

3   See the judgment of Chief Master Hurst in the Claims Direct Test Cases: Tranche 2 issues (3 January 2003).

6

Managing people – the framework

After a look at some general and strategic issues of human resources management, this chapter turns to examine the processes and perils of recruiting staff. This is then tied into the need for a staff induction programme, and the opportunity it offers to initiate the ways in which goals can be set and performance reviewed and appraised, for both staff and partners. Target setting and performance review are considered in some detail. The consequences of performance reviews for planning and evaluating training are then discussed. The chapter moves on to issues relating to communication and the more personal issues that managers may encounter. In particular, the challenges of effective teamworking are discussed. Finally, some tips are given on how to deal with the situation where grievance or disciplinary issues arise.

Introduction

The importance of good 'people management'

One of the first areas where a new partner may expect to acquire hands-on management obligations and experience is in the sphere of 'people management'. Indeed, it is probably in this skill that he is most likely to have had to flex his wings before acquiring partnership status – perhaps in the management of a team within his department, or in conducting project-oriented team development. At a micro level, he will have needed to build a working relationship with his secretary and those immediately around him. He should not be tempted to rest on his laurels, however, since this aspect of professional life is one where skills need to be augmented throughout a career, and where the next surprise is forever only just around the corner.

Three aspects of people management

The management of people within a law firm cannot be seen as a united whole, for there are at least three different perspectives which are important. The first, and the most obvious, is the management of staff by the new partner, to whom such tasks will be delegated either formally, or by virtue of staff expectations of his new role. The second, and perhaps less obvious, area is the management of his fellow partners, not in a sense (in the early days at least) of exercising control over them, but rather of being able to anticipate and condition their expectations of him, and thus being able to influence their management of him. The third, which impacts heavily on the first two, but is probably thought about the least, is the partner's management of himself, i.e. developing and controlling behavioural and attitudinal patterns which will facilitate the achievement of the first two objectives. The new partner must recognise that his new role is so different from that which has gone before that previously acceptable and indeed beneficial approaches may no longer be apt or adequate.

The role of systematic management

The central nature of human resources management is recognised by all the formal recognition standards for systematic or quality management reviewed in Chapter 3, i.e. the Law Society's 'Lexcel'; the CLS 'Specialist Quality Mark', and the generally applicable ISO 9000 (2001). Further, it has a standard all of its own, the government backed 'IIP'. These all cover the same basic areas, but approach them in different ways. Thus they all provide systems for recruitment, induction, training, informing, appraising, etc. None, however, covers reward structures directly, presumably since the individuality of this is accepted. Where they differ is in the ways in which they monitor the effectiveness of such systems and the firm's compliance with them. Lexcel still requires written evidence of documented procedures. However, other standards have increasingly moved away from this emphasis on documentation, and towards a reliance upon evidence from discussions with the staff themselves of the effectiveness of the system, i.e. to a focus more on outcomes than on procedures. Whether those outcomes can in practice be achieved without a documented procedure to back them up is questionable, but an emphasis on whether systems work, as opposed to merely whether they exist, is generally welcome.

Management of staff – general

Differentiating management and persuasion

In similar fashion to the split looked at above, there are two major facets to the management of staff. The first is the formal management techniques as applied to human resource management, from induction onwards. These are the building blocks of good staff management. The second is the art of persuasion of staff (and others) within the context of team working and change management. These latter topics are dealt with later in this chapter and in Chapter 9. The new partner is as likely to be a member of a team as to be its controller, and as likely to be the subject of change as to be its proponent. For instance, one could apply all the sophisticated team building techniques available, but they will be to no avail if those who are drafted onto the team do not feel that they are part of the team, or are not trained to be able to contribute to it, and do not appreciate where it fits in terms of the firm's objectives and strategy.

Tying people management to the firm's strategy and culture

When considering what approach to bring to all aspects of the human resources management programme, it is essential to remember to deploy the techniques available so as to emphasise, and not conflict with, the general strategy and culture of the firm. Thus, to be simplistic, it is no good training a member of staff in, say, family work, if the firm's strategy is to concentrate on institutional rather than private client work. Nor is it any good, at induction, telling a new recruit what a friendly and open place the firm is to work in, if the reality is that that the culture of the firm is formal and even antagonistic. That it is possible to get the approach right is shown by the fact that several law firms feature regularly in the annual survey carried out by *The Times* of the 100 best UK companies to work for. It takes thought, time and effort to get it right and this is plain to any who have encountered dissatisfied staff and failing firms.

The partner/manager's role as employment lawyer

Nowadays, with so much specialisation within the legal profession, comparatively few lawyers would see themselves as specialists in the field of employment law. With the plethora of home-grown statutes and regulations, and EU Directives, together with developments in case law at both domestic and EU level, this is one of the fastest-changing landscapes in the legal world. This does not mean to say, however, that a partner who is not an employment specialist can abrogate all responsibility to his specialist colleagues. He must visualise himself as a manager of a business unit, and consider what level of knowledge such a manager, whether in a professional service firm or a manufacturing company, should apply before calling in the business's external legal advisers. There is a temptation to consider that, because specialist advice is available without direct cost from in-house colleagues, a partner needs to apply less thought to the legal situation in the first place than would a business manager, and therein lies the danger.

Many employment law problems arise from relatively low level management decisions: a slip in recruitment procedures; a badly handled request for flexible working from a woman returning from maternity leave; tolerance of attitudes which are no longer acceptable, etc. These are not situations where the employment lawyers are likely to be called in, at least until the damage is done and the battle lines are drawn. Each partner needs therefore to maintain sufficient working knowledge of the practices and parameters of employment law to ensure that, at the very least, when confronted with a decision with employment law implications, the warning signs are noted, allowing him to take the necessary technical advice.

Recruitment

General

Nowhere is the need for a working knowledge of employment law more demonstrably true than at the stage of recruitment, where the traps for the unwary are legion. Although the applicability of the various statutory and professional discrimination codes will not be discussed here, it is necessary to point out in general terms the stages which any robustly self-protective recruitment process will have to go through.

Choosing the pool

The pool from which recruits are selected, and thus the criteria which are applied, must not be in any way directly or indirectly discriminatory. Thus it has been suggested that the practice of the major firms in selecting their trainees from those with at least a 2:1 degree from a 'good' university, however much they state that they do not discriminate according to, e.g. race amongst that pool, will be indirectly discriminatory. That pool will contain a lower than demographically average proportion of individuals from ethnic minorities. Whether this objection is sustainable or not, such issues need to be considered at the outset, long before the recruitment process goes public.

When choosing where to look for recruits, managers should be careful to ensure that both active efforts (such as visiting universities) and passive ones (such as advertising) are planned so as to reach as wide a range of prospective candidates as possible. Similarly, personal recommendations (from family or friends) should be regarded as potentially dangerous as they may attract only those who mirror the firm's current demographic and ethnographic profile.

Getting the paperwork right

There are several stages of paperwork involved in the recruitment process, which may or may not be assisted by external agencies or consultancies. The importance of getting these processes correct is heightened by Part 1 of the Employment Practices Data Protection Code, a non-statutory but nonetheless highly persuasive code issued by the Information Commission under the Data Protection Act 1998. All recruitment paperwork should be internally coherent. The initial advertisement should indicate as clearly as possible what the job will entail and what criteria will govern the selection process. Use of an application form is advised as an alternative to inviting the submission of CVS, since it offers the opportunity to eliminate unnecessary and potentially dangerous information which might be thought to be discriminatory. The form should be designed to tease out those qualities and criteria on which selection will be based. Applicants should be told what organisation is handling their information and how it will be dealt with, unless this is clear from the advertisement or application form. Candidates should be told of any verification processes that will be used.

Shortlisting

Shortlisting should be carried out in accordance with pre-set and non-discriminatory tests agreed at the start of the process. If an automated system is to be used, e.g a points scoring system, candidates should be told of this. However, a simple decision to exclude, say, all applicants without a degree would not trigger this requirement. Notes of shortlisting decisions should concentrate on objective criteria and avoid extraneous criteria creeping in. Thus, taking the example of the practice of firms noted above, it is no use inviting applications from students at all universities, if only those from 'good' universities will be selected at the shortlisting stage.

Interviewing practices and techniques

Interviewing is not, for most people, an instinctive or innate skill. The interview is an artificial environment where many feel uncomfortable. More attention seems to be given to the skills needed to be a good interviewee than those required for the interviewer. In many cases, some training in interview techniques for new partners is a valuable and productive investment. It is recommended that interviews should not be conducted by one person only. This would waste an invaluable opportunity for at least two people to form an opinion of the candidate. In addition, use of two interviewers helps both to eliminate, and to provide evidence of the elimination of, any discriminatory slant to the interview. Questions should focus on the key criteria and on a clearly framed job description which should be disclosed to the candidate either at the start of the interview or beforehand. If possible, questions should be based on a pre-prepared script. Any attempt to go beyond that factual matrix, e.g. for the perfectly valid reason of seeing how a candidate presents as an advocate of a reasoned argument, should be initiated by open rather than leading questions. The records of the interview should focus on the same sets of data, and should be set out in as objective a form as possible (e.g. score sheets).

Post interview

Once the selection process is complete, the candidates should be told the outcome as soon as possible. If the selected candidate does not accept the post, other potential candidates should be notified of their position. Good practice suggests that candidates should be informed in writing that they will, upon request, be given written reasons as to why they did not succeed. The reason for this is twofold. First it assists the candidates with future interview situations by informing them of hurdles they did not clear and might wish to review; and second it avoids, in situations where there is a genuine and justifiable reason why a candidate from, say, an ethnic background was not selected, a lingering belief that the real reason for failure was discriminatory. Any internal memos or e-mails (all of which are potentially disclosable in any subsequent tribunal proceedings) should be written with an eye to these issues. All paperwork should be carefully preserved for a predetermined period after the recruitment process is completed, to allow any potential claims to be defended. The period should be one which meets the needs of the business.

Induction of staff into the firm

General

Induction of new employees is a multi-layered process. Many of these layers will also apply to internally transferred staff. Induction is an excellent opportunity to ensure that staff are 'on-side' from the outset, but this is often neglected. Many firms have no set induction process, or pay lip service only to the process, and what actually happens is casual, rushed and inadequate. Induction should be a carefully structured plan to convey selected information to the newcomer, which will create the right first impression, upon which the firm can thereafter successfully build. It therefore requires time spent in advance to plan the process, and subsequently time invested in the execution of that plan to ensure that it is effective. It will repay that investment of time, as the new recruit will settle into his new environment more rapidly, and will soon be able to work efficiently within the new setting. This applies across the board, from informal information (the location of nearest bank and shops) to formal information (lines of communication and responsibility).

Induction to the infrastructure of the firm

At its most basic, induction will need to deal with: the physical environment of the firm, e.g. safety drills and features; IT and other systems; and organisation of personnel. This may well be done away from the operational departments, e.g. by a personnel manager. The partner in charge of the newcomer needs however to ensure that the process is effective, and that the new member of his team has, right from the outset, the information he needs to operate. This stage is often neglected when temporary staff are hired. If they have not visited the firm before, and are not given at least these basic levels of induction, they may spend much of their time pestering their permanent colleagues with questions of the 'How do you do this round here?' variety.

Introduction to operational aspects of the role

The responsible partner is almost certain to be involved in the induction of the new staff member when it comes to the operational aspects of the job. Inevitably, for most posts, a degree of technical competence will be assumed to have been a requirement before recruitment. This may not be the case in training posts, but even here any necessary personal skills and qualifications should have been verified at the recruitment stage. In practice, however careful the recruitment efforts, it is not always possible to get the choice right. Part of the role of the responsible partner is thus to ensure that the right information and assistance is given to the newcomer to allow him to demonstrate whether he is indeed sufficiently competent. The partner must avoid making an early unfavourable assessment if the reality is that it is an information deficiency, rather than technical incompetence, that produces poor early performance. Conversely, if all requisite information is properly given, and if the employee still does not perform adequately, then the ability to spot this at an early stage is very valuable. A decision can then be made as to whether additional training will fill any gaps, or whether an early parting of company is advisable.

Establishing the aspirations of the firm and of the new employee

The third aspect of induction is to ensure an exchange of aspirational information. In other words the newcomer needs to be told, in the depth appropriate to the post, the firm's plans for the future, and the goals set for the unit within the firm in which the newcomer is to be placed. He also needs to know what the firm's expectations of him will be in moving towards those goals, and what his own targets (and how they are to be measured) will be. Equally, the partners should gain some idea of the individual's own aspirations in terms of desired competencies, career progression, etc. Again, the earlier any divergences in expectation can be identified, the better. Thus, if a newly appointed assistant solicitor will be unhappy unless he makes partner in four years, and those responsible for him know there is no chance of this happening for at least ten years, this should be addressed sooner rather than later. The induction stage should be regarded as being the first, integral, part of the firm's staff appraisal processes, and not as a stand alone exercise.

Goal setting and reviews

Interim review

The mutual exchange of information which began with the induction process will continue on an informal daily basis as the new employee settles into his role. It is a good idea to have some kind of semi-formal progress review after, say, six months. For those firms which use a probationary period, this will be the opportunity to assess whether the new employee has passed. Again, the process is a reciprocal one. The partner responsible will want to know any areas where the employee still feels unsure and any areas where there may be problems. The employee, on the other hand, will be keen (often to a much larger extent than the employer realises) to have some feedback on how his contribution is being rated. Any new employee will have a basic sense of insecurity, and this is an ideal chance of either providing reassurance that all is well, or pointing out areas where there are problems, so that the relevant issues can be addressed, whether by changes in his personal approach or by undertaking further training. If this is not done, there is a real chance of the employer becoming increasingly concerned about problems of which the employee may be genuinely and blissfully unaware.

Establishing goals and targets

All of this is part of an essential – and continually developing – process of establishing the goals towards which the employee is agreed to be aiming. The same applies to the newly promoted partner. In practice, the difference may be that, even in firms that have well-developed systems for staff, there is nothing like a parallel application of systems for partners. In such circumstances, the new partner has to take the initiative to establish what is actually expected of him.

The target setting process should involve a two-way exercise in assessing:

- the firm's various needs, e.g. productivity;
- the individual's skills as they currently exist;
- the effect of agreed training;
- the resources available; and
- the use of the particular goal as a stepping stone towards longer-term aspirations.

Agreeing targets and measuring performance

Firms will want to set targets that stretch the individual, whereas the individual may be more cautious as to what he can actually achieve. This gives rise to tensions that are inevitably inherent in the process. The key is that if the target is to be useful to both sides, i.e. a realistic estimate from the firm's viewpoint of what it can expect from the individual, and an attainable mark which will give real satisfaction to him when achieved, then it must be an agreed position. An example of what can happen if things go wrong is given in the box below. Further, any target should be capable of objective measurement, where possible. It will not always be feasible, however, to use only objective measures. Indeed, it can be undesirable for there to be too much concentration on one or two issues. Law firms are notorious for their concentration on fees billed and chargeable hours recorded. Where the development of individuals is concerned, i.e. in the stages where they are being considered for partnership or have recently attained that status, there are other skills, such as marketing abilities, which are not as easily quantified and are still important to the firm.

An example of the perils of getting it wrong occurred in 2002 in a memo from the American associates of one of the world's largest law firms, Clifford Chance LLP, who had been set a target of 2,420 chargeable hours per annum. Among the comments this generated were: that such targets were profoundly unrealistic; dehumanising; verging on abdication of professional responsibilities; encouraging padding of hours, inefficient work and repetition of tasks; and leading senior assistants to retain work that they should have passed to their juniors. The result of the furore was that the firm, in the glare of publicity, dropped the whole concept of billable hours' targets. How much better it would have been if they had chosen, in the first place, targets which were realistically attainable within the bounds of the proper professional conduct of work, and which their associates could have taken a pride in achieving. The same goes for any targets.

Appraisals

General

Appraisals of employees have become a common part of the landscape during the last decade. There is growing appreciation of the fact that, unless there is a formally created opportunity for discussion, there are many things which will not be expressed. This is not to refute the idea that there should be a continuous dialogue between individuals and their managers, for which the appraisal is a highlight. There are however still great variations amongst firms in how appraisals are approached, the extent to which they are taken seriously and actually used as a business tool (as opposed to being regarded as a necessary evil required for retaining a badge such as Lexcel or IIP), and the place (if any) of appraisals of partners.

Appraisal methods

Most firms will have appraisal systems which have evolved over time. In some ways this is desirable, since it can be seen to be a sensible process of development based on experience. If, however, the process is merely reactive. it will not be doing its proper job, which needs to be tied into the firm's strategy.

Those responsible for the appraisal system need to sit down and think what they actually want the process to achieve. Is it, for instance, to be solely an assessment of how the appraisee has performed against metrics such as fees billed, and what can be done to improve this? Or, at the opposite end of the spectrum, is it to look solely at issues such as the appraisee's aspirations, desired training, frustrations with the firm, etc.? There is no 'one-size fits all' solution, but, generally, neither extreme is appropriate. Only in some respects, for instance, will any system of 'scoring' the appraisee be appropriate: e.g. it is possible to score the number of chargeable hours recorded, but it is impossible to score career aspirations. The firm should be attempting to assess how the appraisee is doing, and how he can be anticipated to improve, i.e. how can he help the firm to achieve its targets, in a way which also gives personal satisfaction and fits with career ambitions. What can the firm do, e.g. in terms of resources and training, to promote those mutually beneficial achievements?

The partner's role

Most firms' appraisal systems will involve the appraisee's line manager as a key part of the process. This may mean that the line manager is solely responsible for conducting and documenting the appraisal, or, if this will be done by someone else, that the line manager's preliminary input by way of his assessment of the appraisee is central. The newly elevated partner is likely to find himself, perhaps for the first time, in the position of line manager, and taking a crucial role in a process which he has previously only experienced from the other side of the desk. Only a lucky few find appraisals an instinctively easy task, and for most, some training in conducting appraisal interviews is highly advantageous. Most sensible firms will provide this, whether by making use of training courses, or by use of video training aids. The difficulty is giving the interview a structure and a purpose, while at the same time creating a comfortable and open atmosphere in which the appraisee will feel free to discuss his perception of the firm in a creative and constructive manner. If not offered by the firm, the new partner should seek out such training.

Avoiding a threatening position

One of the essentials of the appraisal process is that the appraisee should not be made to feel under threat. There will inevitably be a degree of nervousness, if the process is to be thorough, as it is only human to be concerned as to what perceptions may be held by others. One of the areas which may cause difficulty is any linkage between the review process and the firm's salary reviews. Most firms prefer to separate the two, although if the review is a genuine attempt to assess how well the individual is doing it would be naïve to think that it will not form part of the salary decision. Another generally accepted tenet is that there should be no surprises sprung on the appraisee at interview. That means that the comments of all those who are asked to contribute to the review should be gathered and passed on to the appraisee before the interview. This gives the appraisee the chance to prepare his response to any criticism. It will be the task of the line manager to ensure that any resultant tensions are minimised, whether these are between him and the appraisee, or between the appraisee and others whose contributions have been sought.

The 360° approach

Who should be involved in the apparaisal process? At its simplest, it can merely involve the appraiser and the appraisee. Normally (and preferably) the appraiser will be the line manager with immediate responsibility for the appraisee, and will not necessarily be a partner. Unless the line manager and appraiser are one and the same person, then whichever is undertaking the interview will need the views of the other, and these should be circulated as mentioned above. It is possible for more than one person to act as appraiser, but generally this will be too heavy a commitment of time, and too heavy-handed an approach to find favour.

The other question is whether the views of those who report to the appraisee should also be sought. The preferable view is that they should, as this can add value to the process and because the appraisal process should be as open as possible. This is known as a 360° approach. Thus a secretary will be best placed to say whether, for instance, her boss is a good time manager, and thus able to make best use of the time available to both of them. She will also be most directly able to comment on how well his client relationships and file management are conducted, e.g. is there a problem with file overload, and consequently a pattern of unanswered telephone calls? This can be an essential early warning system. Equally, with a more senior fee earner responsible for supervising others, soliciting the views of those to whom he delegates work will give a picture of how efficient his supervision is, which again gives the firm warning of where problems may arise in this claim-sensitive area. The 360° approach does involve more commitment of resources, but its potential benefits are great.

Taking appraisals seriously

For many firms, their first exposure to appraisal systems will not have been entirely voluntary. That is to say that they will first have ventured into them in response to the requirements of an external auditing body, with the condition that the firm have a documented system of appraisals. Having passed the audit, there is a temptation to relax, and to think that going through the motions will be sufficient to get the firm through any subsequent reassessment for the quality mark.

There are two reasons why this temptation should be resisted. The first is that many of the quality assessment bodies have changed their approach. They are no longer satisfied by, or even require, the existence of a documented appraisal system. What they require, and what they will test by interviews with staff, is that there is in place a working, effective, appraisal system. Lip service will not suffice. The second reason for not adopting such an approach is that it wastes an invaluable business opportunity. It is a truism that law firms are 'people-based' businesses – but this is nonetheless true! Appraisals offer a chance to review, and communicate the firm's message, in a way which is directly relevant to the individual, in respect of many areas of the appraisee's and the firm's operations. Many of these are items which simply will not crop up in the ordinary course of the working day, and may be areas which people will find it easier to pass by rather than to confront. A non-exhaustive list of the areas for discussion would be:

- the appraisee's career and other aspirations;
- whether those match the firm's plans for him;
- if not, whether the two aspects can be reconciled;
- what training may be needed to progress agreed development;
- how the appraisee copes with the interpersonal demands of his job;

- how he copes with the self-management requirements, e.g. time management;
- how the appraisee is perceived by those around him;
- his record in terms of sickness and attendance;
- whether he has any relevant personal problems which have adversely affected his performance;
- how these may relate to, and be capable of improvement by, work-related changes;
- how the appraisee is performing against 'hard' measures such as billing;
- what can be done to improve performance;
- what resources may be needed to help in that improvement.

Extending the appraisal system to partners

A number of firms which have successfully introduced staff appraisal schemes have either baulked at, or had considerable problems with, the extension of appraisals to partners. Not all systems require partners to be covered, for example Lexcel, although the CLS Specialist Quality Mark and Investors in People do. A number of problems are perceived as follows:

- *Partners resent being appraised by their equals, and even more so by those whom they may consider as juniors.* The plain fact is that all partners are appraised continuously by their partners, whatever their status in the pecking order. Having a formal system gives this some accept-able form, and should help to minimise the build-up of hidden resentments which are potentially more damaging than open discussion.
- *Partners may have hidden agendas, and allow these to influence their judgement as appraisers.* This may on occasions be true. To overcome this, involving more than one appraiser may be appropriate. Some firms may even wish to involve third parties, external to the firm, as part of the process.
- *A partner's job requires much that is not capable of being objectively measured.* This is true, but should only pose a problem in those firms that have not sat down to address the fundamental questions of what they believe they are there for, i.e. what behaviours, skills and per-formance levels are expected of a partner, and how these relate to the ambitions of the firm. It could be suggested that a firm which cannot articulate those matters in order to formulate an appraisal scheme, is a firm that does not know where it wants to go or how it wishes to get there, and has a problem in business planning terms which goes far beyond appraisal difficulties.

- *The time commitment is too great.* Undeniably, there are time implications, especially if dual appraisers are used. Looked at another way, however, what more important task could there be for partners than to review the role that each is playing in the progress of the firm, and their ideas for the development of their own place within the firm? Used properly, such interviews could, for instance, form the basis for the conduct of the firm's strategic review, or partners' away-days.

The 360° approach to appraisals for partners

If ever there is a case for taking the 360° approach to appraisals, it is with regard to partners. Because the range of their responsibilities is so much greater than others, and the scope of their interactions within and without the firm is so much wider, it is vital to adopt a procedure that involves ascertaining the views of a wide range of those who may be considered as stakeholders in the partners' performance. A partner's abilities, qua partner, cannot be assessed in terms only of his fee-earning, for instance. Some of the largest firms have now recognised this to the extent that they undertake partner assessments (not necessarily annual) which are conducted on their behalf by external organisations, and which include involving a range of participants, including e.g.:

- clients;
- suppliers of linked professional services;
- counsel; and
- relevant professional associations.

Training

General

Like many professions, the training of a lawyer is heavily front-loaded. The initial training he receives, whether it be the academic experience of a law or other degree; the more practical courses of the Common Professional Examination and the Legal Practice Course; or the hands-on experience of a training contract, is by far the greatest part of any lawyer's training. Indeed, it was only comparatively recently that senior solicitors were brought into the regime for compulsory Continuing Professional Development (CPD) training.

A disregard for the importance of continuing training still informs, to a potentially dangerous degree, the thinking of some within the profession, especially at the more senior end, who often control training expenditure. A potential partner will therefore do well to assess his firm's attitude to training when considering whether this is a place where he (and those working with him) will be able fully to develop during their working careers.

Formulating a training plan

All the relevant quality assurance standards require the firm to have a training plan, so that training is planned rather than haphazard. Formulating this plan should not be an arduous task if the firm's appraisal scheme is working efficiently. That process should reveal agreed training requirements in accordance with the firm's strategy. Further, the timing of training can be crucial – there is no point in attending a course if it will be months or years before the opportunity to put it into practice will arise, as the information gained will simply be forgotten. The purpose of the training plan, therefore, is to draw those threads together: to assess if individual training wishes can be granted; to discover any gaps which will need to be addressed for the overall strategic plan of the firm to be fulfilled; to apply budgetary controls to the process; and to offer a framework for the selection of the most appropriate form of training for each need.

Available training methods

Fortunately, there is a growing range of training methods available. Many people, when they think of training, think mainly of external and remote events, whether these be conferences, courses or seminars. While these may be effective, they can also be expensive, geographically remote, and unacceptably time-consuming. If possible, their use should be restricted to occasions when either the range of topics presented, or the expertise of the presenter(s) cannot be replicated, or when the networking opportunities may be valuable. Where face-to-face presentations are considered necessary, they may be more accessible through in-house courses where a larger group of staff will benefit. They may also be arranged by combining with other interested firms in the locality, or using the facilities of local law societies, many of which have very well developed programmes.

A growing number of other approaches are available and recognised by the Law Society's CPD requirements, such as:

- Video and TV based training, from specialist suppliers either of commercially-oriented or specifically legal videos.
- On-line training, now including the development of real-time virtual conferencing.
- Training based around publications, from informal reading and research to the more formal correspondence course.
- Training conducted by others within the firm, as an adjunct not only to the improvement of knowledge of the recipient, but also the professional development of the presenter. This may be particularly

appropriate for the situation where one team member researches new legislation which will be relevant to the whole team.

The scope of training

Reference has been made to the proverbially parsimonious attitude of some firms to their training budgets. This often relates to the specific topic for which training is sought. Thus, while a firm may support 'black-letter law' training, i.e. technical training such as 'Changes in conveyancing practice' or 'A personal injury update', it may be more reluctant to pay for training designed to address the personal needs of employees. Training in the so-called 'soft skills', e.g. time management, teamwork building, controlling stress, supervision and delegation skills, etc., may remain difficult to obtain. The new partner should therefore be particularly watchful of the firm's practice in this regard if he wants to be able to develop his and his team's skills in broad terms.

Reiterative training

Another barometer to the firm's attitude to training is its approach to reiterative training, i.e. the reinforcement of previous training by further training in the same field. The classic area in which this is often necessary – but seldom given – is in the IT sphere. Training in the use of a new software programme is often given by someone who is so familiar with the package, or whose manual and keyboard dexterity are such, that the training is too fast for the trainees. Some find it harder to keep up than others but do not want to appear foolish by asking questions.

If a firm is serious about getting the most out of IT, it should offer what has been called 'relentless training' as a follow-up. This should not be available on a demand only basis, as that will catch only those who are willing. Instead, it should be given on a compulsory basis, to ensure that all are operating at full competence. Every partner should continually assess whether every member of his team is operating at an acceptable level and has received sufficient training for the purpose.

The follow-up to training

One of the biggest lessons learned by those who implemented Investors in People as a standard was that their systems of follow-up from training were often inadequate (if not non-existent). Three problems may result from this. First, there is no means of applying, on any future training purchase, the lessons which the individual trainee may have learned from his experience. He may, for instance, have found the training company's efficiency, or the presenter's skills, or the venue's suitability, particularly good or bad. Unless centrally recorded and readily available, this knowledge, which could affect profoundly the value that the firm is likely to gain from a similar subsequent purchase, will be lost.

Second, unless the knowledge gained is distributed within the firm by the trainee, and somehow retained within the firm's knowledge database, only the individual trained will benefit, and the wider personnel within the firm will know nothing of the exercise. Thus, returning trainees should be required to brief all others who might benefit, by presentation and/or by notes, on the content of the training, and to deposit centrally or otherwise make readily available the written element of the course. Third, unless applied, the knowledge gained will be lost, at least partially. The presentation/notes referred to above will help to fix the information in the trainee's head, but ideally both he and his supervisor should actively seek work which will offer him the chance to implement his new skills. The partner should seek to ensure that all the steps described above are taken by the recipient of the training as soon as is possible after the training experience, while all is still fresh in the mind.

Monitoring the CPD requirements

In many firms, the direct responsibility for monitoring the compliance of personnel with CPD requirements will be centrally organised by the training partner or the HR manager. It is suggested, however, that it is prudent for each partner to be familiar with these records insofar as the personnel within their own department are concerned. The reasons for this are threefold. First, it is not safe to assume that all concerned will remember or understand the requirements, even though it is the personal obligation of every solicitor under the Practising Certificate Regulations. By keeping a weather eye on individuals, partners can ensure that the regulations are being complied with, and can also help their staff by encouraging them to record qualifying work (e.g. time spent in legal research) which they may not realise is recordable. Second, it should help to plan the timing of training so as to smooth out peaks and troughs with regard to both the time and monetary commitments of the department. Third – and all the more important now that the regulations are based on annual (rather than triennial) targets – it will help to avoid any last minute panics. Anecdotal evidence from another profession (chartered surveyors) suggests that externally contracted compliance auditors have frequently found, and pursued, instances of failure to comply with CPD requirements, both in terms of having the training and recording that training. As the Law Society's Practice Standards Unit teams gain impetus, it can be assumed that this will be an area they are keen to monitor.

Training for support staff

Much of what has been written above will be applicable to professionally qualified staff, or at least those with fee-earning responsibilities. That should not be taken as suggesting that the training of support staff should be given any less priority. Again, these needs should be recognised as part of the appraisal process. These may be wide ranging, as with an IT manager's need to keep up with technical developments, or an HR manager's requirement to keep abreast of employment law. On the other hand they may be more restrictive, e.g. a secretary's need to become familiar with a software package. Nor should the need for 'soft skills' training be ignored, e.g. the need for receptionists to be trained in handling awkward callers, or for secretaries to have a grasp of time management techniques.

Working together

Introduction to working together

This section of this chapter looks at the requirements for managing the ways in which those within a firm should work together, and what the new partner's role(s) will be in this process. There is a good deal of overlap with the following section, which looks at teamworking as a specific subject, but this section is intended to address the more general issues, rather than the specific issues which emerge in the context of, for instance, an ad hoc, project-related team.

The central place of communication

Those who undertake MBA studies will be offered a variety of diagrammatically-based models showing different approaches that they may apply to decision-taking. Central to all of these models is the requirement for the manager to identify those groups who have a stake in the relevant decision, i.e. those who may play a role in the taking of the decision in either an active sense, by participating in the decision-taking process; or passively, in that their reaction to it can affect its success or failure. This serves to emphasise in all cases the central importance of good communications, in both directions. Thus, the timing and manner of the communication of a decision to a group, e.g. informing the secretaries in a department of a decision to purchase a case management system, can be just as important as seeking the views of a group, such as that department's senior assistants, who may have been actively involved in the procurement process. Unfortunately, law firms, as a generality, are notorious for allowing poor communications, often with the spurious excuse that the individual involved was too busy with client work. Anecdotal evidence abounds of events such as the staff of a firm who learned of an agreed merger by reading about it in the local paper. The point – easy to state but potentially difficult to implement – is that part of the process in arriving at and implementing any decision has to be a consideration of:

- Who needs to be asked for input to the process?
- Who will be affected by the decision?
- How, and equally important, when should each identifiable group be told of the decision?

The new partner's position

One of the major changes in a new partner's position will be his place in the communication chain. There will be a variety of ways in which this will show itself. For a start, he will become party to a great deal of information, to which he will not previously have had access. This may be from the firm's accounts, attendance at partners' meetings, and being privy to discussions between partners. What is more, it will be assumed by staff that he has access to all such information, even if in practice he does not, e.g. because it is confined to a committee of partners rather than shared amongst all the partnership. He will find himself having to make judgements as to what information he is able to share with those who, until a short while ago, were his fellow employees or even his contemporaries. He will be acutely aware that, if he makes a wrong decision in this respect, his new partners will take a dim view of his actions. He should not therefore be afraid to seek guidelines from them as to how to handle the situation. Further, there will be a number of instances in which it is a positive part of his role to handle communications which have to be made, and he should ensure that he is properly equipped to do this fully and in a timely fashion. Instead of being merely the recipient of information, he will have a major part to play as a conveyor of it.

'Management by walking about'

There are many managers who will state that the most important part of their role falls under the title of 'Management By Walking About', i.e. that communication is not something restricted to structured events, but is a daily, informal, exchange of information on all relevant subjects. While this is a highly desirable state of affairs, the hard fact is that for most new partners it will need to be combined with a major fee-earning load and so, for reasons of time management, may need to be restricted to the teams within which they work. The point is that an open and approachable style should be developed, combined with an ability to set time aside for concentration without being disturbed.

Means of internal communication

Bilateral discussions may be the most desirable means of communicating anything within an office environment, but they are very time consuming and simply not effective when information needs to be communicated to a large number of people. There are, however, a wide range of options which can be deployed, and often the partners will have to decide which is the most effective and acceptable.

Staff meetings

Staff meetings will broadly fall under two headings. First, it is common practice for an operational division which is small enough to conduct informal meetings, to do so on a regular basis, simply to review progress at an operational level. Any one person may be a member of a number of such divisions, e.g. an employment solicitor might regularly attend litigation department meetings, but also those of an ad hoc commercial team put together for a major project; or a secretary might attend meetings both of the conveyancing department and all the secretaries in the private client department. Such meetings will normally need only a rough agenda, and the level of discussion may vary from consideration of changes in the law for the relevant field, through a review of departmental workloads, to a look at individual cases of major import.

The second type of meeting will be where it is appropriate for all, or a selected group of staff, to be called to a meeting to discuss major events or decisions. Often, in such cases, staff will prefer a face-to-face presentation, even if this needs to be preceded or followed by written information for them to consider. Such events are likely to follow a more formal pattern, with a set agenda, but should wherever possible allow for questions and comments from the floor, rather than being merely a one-sided presentation.

Staff liaison committees

Many firms will develop some form of standing body as a means of communication between staff and partners. For want of a better term, this is referred to here as a staff liaison committee. The aim is to ensure that all sections of staff, from all departments at all levels (not forgetting the administrative staff) have a regular opportunity to meet with partners to discuss a range of issues. Firms may decide to exclude some areas from discussion, e.g. salaries or comments about individuals. There will usually be some form of informal election or choice of the staff representatives. If possible, the staff themselves should be encouraged to play as active a part as possible in the administration of the meetings, e.g. by setting the agenda, chairing the meetings, writing and distributing the minutes, etc.

The minutes need to be public for the exercise to succeed. The role of the partners is to make sure that the administration does work effectively, that meetings do not descend into trivia and that all concerned get a reasonable chance to express their views. Partners should be open to consideration of sensible points raised. After the meeting, the partners should ensure that points which need consideration are dealt with without undue delay, that ideas are incorporated where possible (with credit being given where due), and that a clear and reasoned response is given to all points. If the staff feel that only lip service is being paid to the meetings, i.e. all suggestions made are habitually rejected, then the meetings will end up being counterproductive.

Firms which are alive to changes in employment law may look to reshape these committees over the next few years, to be ready to comply with the Information and Consultation Directive. This must be given legislative force by the UK government by 2005, and will require elected representatives of the staff in certain circumstances to act as a channel of communication for the consideration and implementation of important business decisions.

Written communications

Whether these consist of paper memos or e-mails, written communications should be kept to a minimum, as it is easy for overload to set in. It will rarely be appropriate for memos, etc. to be the only means of communication for any matter of importance. They will be most appropriate if they are communicating information which is time-sensitive, flagging up something which will be reinforced by other supplemental forms of communication, or serving as a permanent record of information needing to be kept for subsequent consultation.

Newsletters

One particular form of written communication is the firm's newsletter. These can vary greatly in both form and intent. Some will give only hard information, but many will be of a more 'chatty' and ephemeral style, dealing with staff comings and goings and staff-related events and achievements. The mixture of information included, and the presentation, will be a matter for each firm to resolve. The chance to use such publications to reinforce information also conveyed by other means should not be ignored, especially if the publication is attractive and one that staff will want to read, and hence one from which they may absorb information that otherwise might pass them by.

Dealing with personal issues

Coping with the role change upon attaining partnership

One potentially difficult transition which the new partner will face is the shift in personal relations between him and the staff around him. This may well be a gradual change, but the fact is that they will have moved from being fellow members of staff, to being his employees. In short, he will have moved from being 'one of us' to 'one of them'. This may, of course, be a perfectly natural experience, but some employees may find the situation difficult. The new partner can of course help to mitigate any potential adverse reaction by the way in which he conducts himself. Care should be taken to avoid any sudden change in attitude, i.e. the new partner needs to be conscious of the need to refrain from demonstrating his new authority by throwing his weight about. Equally, however, he needs to be alert to the fact that some employees may try to take advantage of his new status, by seeking concessions which they know they would not get from a more experienced partner.

Managing confidential information

One instance of this change is that the new partner becomes privy to confidential information about individual members of staff. This may be basic data such as salary levels, or more sensitive information about the employee's personal circumstances. This may come either from his fellow partners, such as the firm's plans for or concerns about an individual, or direct from the employee. It may well be that employees will entrust the partner with personal information which they would not have dreamed of passing to a fellow employee. In either event, the partner must be careful to apply the same degree of confidentiality that he would to a client's affairs. Indeed, the responsibility is in some ways even higher, since a client's matters may normally be discussed with colleagues. He will need to consider the practical aspects of this obligation, such as ensuring that he has secure storage facilities for any paperwork or computer data concerning staff. He should also bear in mind, and if necessary seek advice on, the application of the Data Protection Act 1998 to such information, and the question of who may have the right to call for access to such data.

Dealing with requests for changes in working practices

The partner may be the recipient of requests for changes in working practices, usually with regard to working times. These may be for a later start or earlier finish, or simply for fewer working hours. Two workers both wanting a reduction in hours may, for instance, come up with a joint request to move onto a job share basis. Often, in a hard-pressed working environment, such changes will be, at the least, inconvenient. They are likely to be made informally, and the partner may be tempted to give an off-the-cuff answer. The same applies, on a lesser scale, to requests for time off.

The temptation to respond quickly should be resisted at all costs, for whether he realises it or not, the partner is instantly plunged into the realms of possible statutory control and the perils of employment tribunal problems if he gets it wrong. He should therefore give himself time to consider and consult. If his inclination is to grant the request, he should consider what effect this may have in the light of previously refused requests, or those which may follow. If inclined to refuse, he needs to think about whether there is any precedent to the contrary, or whether there are any statutory reasons against such a decision. The most perilous area is a request made in connection with a female member of staff who is returning from maternity leave.

There are many legislative provisions which affect decisions on working practices, and the basic principles may be summarised as:

- Take advice from those responsible for the firm's employment practices.
- Do not differentiate between full and part-time workers.
- Do not discriminate on any of the grounds which are prohibited by statute (e.g. sex, race, disability) or by the firm's (or, in default, the Law Society's) equality and diversity policy.
- Be alert to the possibility of indirect discrimination.
- Approach each decision on the basis that there is a statutory leaning towards such requests being granted.
- Only refuse a request if there is no possibility of discrimination, and if there are clear, objective, operational reasons for refusal.

Staff absences

The new partner, especially if he is a team leader, may find that he needs to keep an eye on staff absences. This may well be the ultimate responsibility of others within the firm, such as the staff partner, or the HR manager, but nonetheless he should acquaint himself with the firm's terms of employment and policies. Some firms, for instance, specify that full pay will be applied during a period (or aggregate periods) of absence up to a certain limit. Other firms may fear that policies which allow ten working days to be taken as fully paid sick leave may be taken to be granting the equivalent of two weeks' extra holiday. Some firms offer no contractual entitlement to paid sick leave at all beyond any statutory sick pay payable, but use their discretion to allow payment in what they consider to be genuine cases. This has to be balanced against the dangers of causing upset if the staff perception is that discretion has been used inconsistently, or to the unfair benefit/detriment of individuals. It should not, however, be assumed that staff are always sympathetic to the absences of their colleagues, particularly if they are under more pressure as a result. If such discretion on sick pay exists, the partner should be familiar with the firm's experience and policy. He should also consider whether interviews with staff on their return from absence are appropriate.

Analysing staff absences

Absences may be the key to information about more deep-seated problems than may at first be apparent. Put simply, if an individual has four weeks off because of a broken leg, that is easily understandable, and should cause no long-term concerns. If however, someone takes an aggregate of 20 working days of sick leave over a period of a year, that may be a symptom of something more deepseated. The absences could be a result of innumerable possible circumstances. Examples could be:

- The employee is simply taking advantage of a perceived lack of control or enforcement of attendance, perhaps in the belief that this is acceptable behaviour in the eyes of his peers.
- It is an indication of poor morale within the firm, so that staff simply do not like coming to work, and the partners need to address the morale issue by, e.g. improved communications or conditions.
- There is an underlying problem with the employee's domestic position, e.g. unreliable child-care arrangements.
- There are interpersonal difficulties within a department, which the partner as manager of the department needs to address.
- The employee is suffering from stress, due to, e.g. a work overload, and is actually afraid of coming to the office, so that a reallocation of work should be considered.
- There is an underlying medical problem which is not being addressed (but which might, for instance, be capable of being tackled under a private medical scheme offered by the firm).

Although the partner may not be the right person to act on this information, he may well be the person best placed to collect it. He should therefore make sure that, at the very least, he liaises carefully with whoever does have the responsibility for acting on such concerns.

Timekeeping

On a similar theme, the partner needs to be alert to those (generally few) members of staff who will push at the boundaries of timekeeping. He should be alert to the risk of an habitual five minutes late becoming 10, or 15 minutes. A short but firm word to the offender will usually suffice, but saying nothing will exacerbate the problem. Similarly, in these days of no smoking rules in offices, many firms allow, or at least fail to protest about, staff taking 'smoke breaks'. The partner will need to be astute to prevent this privilege being abused.

Teamworking

What constitutes a team?

One of the most frequently voiced untruths in an office environment is 'We work as a team here'. This can mean anything from 'Everyone does what I tell them' to 'No-one actually accepts responsibility for anything around here'. Very rarely does it mean that a team is deliberately put together for a specific project, with thought being given to the different tasks required of the team members, and the skills and inherent talents and attitudes which will be needed. Putting together half-a-dozen litigation lawyers, with similar attitudes and abilities, is no more making up a team than putting 11 left-handed seam bowlers onto a cricket pitch. Often, however, that is precisely what happens in a law firm, and woe betide the partner who is given the joyous task of captaining such a 'team', over whose selection he has exercised no control, but for whose product he is responsible.

Selecting a team

Technical skills

When given the opportunity to pick a team, the idea is to aim for a mix of two elements. The first is the range of technical skills which are needed for the task in hand. This may be a mix of types of legal expertise, as where a team on a takeover will include specialists from the company and commercial, commercial property, tax and employment departments, or it may be a case of combining different levels of skill, so that, for instance, a partner has the assistance of a qualified assistant, a couple of paralegals, and a group of secretaries, all of whom form part of an identifiable unit. Most law firms of any size will be familiar with such concepts, and the newly-appointed partner is likely to have been part of a number of such groups during his career.

Personal attributes of team members

What is much less likely to be considered, however, but which is just as vital to the prospect of success for the team, is getting the mix of personal attributes correct, i.e. the spread of skills and attitudes with which each team member will approach his task. There exists considerable literature on the subject, which makes it clear that the technical mix is not enough on its own. Seminal work in this field was done by R. Meredith Belbin.[1] From a lengthy study at the Administrative Staff College at Henley, he and his colleagues identified eight different classifications of potential team members. Further, they devised a psychometric test which is relatively easy to administer, and which identifies for each person the two most dominant characteristics from amongst those eight classifications. The types, and their attendant strengths and weaknesses, are set out in Figure 6.1.

Using the Belbin classifications

It is easy to see from Figure 6.1 how unlikely it is that all attitudes and aptitudes can be wrapped up in one person. For instance, a 'Plant', with his inclination to disregard practical details, is hardly likely to work as a 'Completer – finisher', with his tendency to worry about small things. Equally, a 'Company worker', with his predictable organising ability, could have as his second most notable characteristic that of a 'Monitor – evaluator' with his prudent judgement and discretion. Further, not every individual will be good at working in teams in any role. Belbin estimated that 30 per cent of the managers he and his team assessed did not show any of the analysed roles' characteristics to a degree which would make them useful team members. Interestingly, he identified that a characteristic of such executives was that they were often promoted beyond their real ability, and tended to change jobs frequently. The key is to try to ensure that all the characteristics outlined in Figure 6.1 are represented within the team, so that all tasks can be accomplished. The reality is that it will be rare for the person(s) choosing a team to have the luxury of psychometric test results available to them, and so this will more probably involve trying to match what is known of the personal characteristics of the prospective members to the above classifications.

The size of teams

However, teams need not comprise as many as eight people. As mentioned, many individuals will demonstrate two of the characteristics identified to a degree which makes them useful for both roles. Analysis of the size of successful teams indicates that, while teams of 10 or 11 may in some cases be successful, the risk of indecision outweighs the benefits of multiple inputs, and that in fact the most successful teams tend to comprise five or six people. Reducing the team below that size can be advantageous if relationships are particularly good, but this tends to produce an intensity and concentration of thought which may be counterproductive.

Type	Typical features	Positive qualities	Allowable weaknesses
Company worker	Conservative, dutiful, predictable	Organising ability, practical common sense, hard-working, self-discipline	Lack of flexibility, unresponsiveness to unproven ideas
Chairman	Calm, self-confident, controlled	A capacity for treating and welcoming all potential contributors on their merits and without prejudice. A strong sense of objectivity	No more than ordinary in terms of intellect or creative ability
Shaper	Highly strung, outgoing, dynamic	Drive and a readiness to challenge inertia, ineffectiveness, complacency or self-deception	Prone to provocation, irritation and impatience
Plant	Individualistic, serious-minded, unorthodox	Genius, imagination, intellect, knowledge	Up in the clouds, inclined to disregard practical details or protocol
Resource investigator	Extroverted, enthusiastic, curious, communicative	A capacity for contacting people and exploring anything new. An ability to respond to challenge	Liable to lose interest once the initial fascination has passed
Monitor – evaluator	Sober, unemotional, prudent	Judgement, discretion, hard-headedness	Lacks inspiration or the ability to motivate others
Team worker	Socially orientated, rather mild, sensitive	An ability to respond to people and to situations, and to promote team spirit	Indecisive at moments of crisis
Completer – finisher	Painstaking, orderly, conscientious, anxious	A capacity for follow-through. Perfectionism	A tendency to worry about small things. A reluctance to 'let go'

Figure 6.1   The Belbin classifications.
Source: Adapted from Belbin, R.M. (1981) '*Management Teams: Why they succeed or fail*' Butterworth Heinemann. Reproduced by permission.

The chair's role

Selecting the team members

One thing that emerges very clearly from the available research is the key role played by the chair of a team. A new partner may well find that his elevation promotes him to this post for the first time. Ideally, the chair will have had a hand in the selection of the team members, and been able to apply the above principles to the choice. Often, however, this will not be so and the chair will simply have to work with the members picked by another. His first task is to try to analyse which tasks, within the remit of the team's operations, can best be taken on by each of its members, in the light of not only their technical skills but also their personal aptitudes. Further, the chair should not be afraid to reshuffle the team's tasks to suit what prove in practice to be the individual members' strengths and weaknesses.

Chairing meetings

There is no doubt that chairing a meeting is an art. It can be taught to an extent, and a number of organisations (notably the Institute of Directors) run successful courses in this respect. Some practical suggestions to ease the task of chairing are made in Chapter 9. Not all individuals, however, will be susceptible to such teaching. Impatience; a wish to dominate proceedings; an inability to judge the timing of interventions so as to move the business forward while allowing reasonable debate – all these will prevent a chair, and hence the team, from operating effectively. In practice, the person chosen for the role is likely to be a strong character, and will want to contribute his own ideas. If, however, it is not possible to persuade others to support those views (or, better still, to adopt and promote them as their own) then the chair should not force them through. All people concerned should know they are encouraged to contribute ideas, and will get a fair hearing. Equally, they should be aware that they will not be able to hector or bully other members, in order to push their own views. Respect for the process of the team's work, as manifested by punctuality, and for its members as individuals, as shown by politeness, a lack of interruption, and a willingness to listen, may all need to be encouraged by the chair. Particularly in a team which crosses the boundaries of conventional grades of seniority, achieving this balance can be a tough task for the chair.

Moving forward the team's business

The chair also needs to bear in mind at all times the overall programme and priorities of the team. Digressions are inevitable within any meeting, and indeed can sometimes be productive and yield imaginative thought which will help on topics other than the one immediately under discussion. Equally, however, they can be a distraction to the real business for which the team has been constituted, and it is the chair's task to keep the team focused. Recognisable and achievable steps on the way to the team's goals should be set by the chair, so that segments of work can be completed and a sense of interim achievement can be fostered. A clear (but not necessarily lengthy) record of the decisions taken, and of the next tasks and meeting arrangements (with responsibilities allocated as appropriate) should be circulated promptly after the meeting. All this will help the team to consider that its work as a cohesive unit has been worthwhile, and to continue its efforts.

Managing the end-game

The chair should also make clear what is the ultimate intent of the team, in terms of what will represent successful completion of its work. It may, of course, be that this is simply a recommendation for decision by others, in which case the completion and publication of the report will be the focus. However, the team itself may have decision-taking powers, and a responsibility for the implementation of its conclusions. Here, the members should be made fully aware of the need to consider all constituencies which may be affected by the decision, and what the team members' individual tasks may be in the implementation of those plans. The chair will wish to ensure that the skills of the Completer-Finisher within the group are properly utilised at this stage.

Grievances and disciplinary matters

Checking the procedures

No matter how well-intentioned or managed a firm may be, there may come the day when a partner gets involved in the grievance and disciplinary procedures which are contractually applicable to any dispute that has arisen. Since mishandling either can lead all too easily to the employment tribunal, it is vital to ensure, before embarking on the substantive part of any enquiry or decision-taking process, that the procedures to be used are known, up-to-date, and actually followed. The first step is to check the document(s) which may govern the procedure, whether this be the employee's contract, a staff manual or handbook, etc. Next, it is important to check that the edition being considered is the correct one. It is not uncommon for a contractually-stated policy to have moved on through various changes which have been announced, e.g. by memo, but which have never been filed with the contract, so that the original document is misleading to a potentially dangerous degree. The last step in this chain of preliminary events is to ensure that whatever edition is internally correct is also externally acceptable, i.e. that it meets the requirements of any statutory or other prescribed process, such as the draft procedures published by the Advisory, Conciliation and Arbitration Service (ACAS) as part of their Code of Practice.[2] If not, thought should be given to amending the firm's procedures to comply with these outside requirements, before going any further. Statutory grievance and disciplinary procedures are being introduced in 2003 under the Employment Act 2002.

Taking advice

Establishing correct and acceptable procedures is only one of a number of matters upon which it may well be necessary for a partner to take specialist advice before proceeding. This may be from internal sources, e.g. the firm's HR manager, if it has one, or by consulting an employment lawyer within the firm. If neither of these resources is available, it may be necessary to take advice from outside the firm. In any event, it is sensible to obtain at least preliminary advice at the outset, since employment law is an extremely fast-changing field of law.

Implementing the procedures

It is often a temptation to consider that it will be easier to deal with disciplinary and grievance matters in an informal way, as this will minimise the confrontational stances that formality may produce. This may be true, but it does not help in the long run if reliance upon the discussions is to be necessary. In other words, if the employee has exercised his right to initiate grievance procedures, as opposed to simply voicing a complaint, or if the firm wishes to be able to refer back to discussions of a disciplinary nature if the problem is not solved, then formality and strict procedural compliance is essential.

Preparing for the disciplinary meeting

The first task is to inform the employee of the proposed arrangements for the meeting. This may seem obvious, but in fact it is easy to fail to make it clear what the nature or scope of discussions is to be. It would be prudent to refer the employee to the procedures under which the meeting is to be conducted. Account has also to be taken of the employee's statutory right to be accompanied by a fellow employee, or a trade union representative (not, it should be noted, by a friend who is not a work colleague, or by a legal representative). Again, advice may be needed for this aspect, e.g. as to what will be the role for the representative. In practice, this requirement often imposes a delay on matters, as time has to be allowed in order to permit anyone accompanying the employee to make arrangements to attend. The intervening time can be used to make sure that all papers which may be needed for the meeting are in order, and that they have been made available to the employee. The employee should not be able to claim later to have been ambushed, by having matters or documents put to him at the meeting of which he had had no previous warning.

Conducting the meeting

An important decision for the firm is who shall conduct the meeting. Often the procedures will dictate who this will be, e.g. the partner who is the employee's line manager. Preferably, the rules should allow for more than one person to represent the firm, not only because two perspectives may bring a greater chance of objectivity, but also because if events do later become public, two witnesses may well be better than one. Save for very small firms, there should be the possibility of an appeal to a more senior person, so the relevant partner should be excluded from the preliminary stages. Full opportunity should be given for the employee or his representative to state his position. It can be a difficult exercise to draw a balance between allowing full enquiry, and treating the meeting like a trial, with the employee wanting to 'call witnesses'. Once again, advice may well be needed in advance as to how the meeting should be conducted in the circumstances of the particular problem. Past events can be considered, but the danger of relying on informal recollection, or notes of complaints not processed properly at the time, or previous warnings which have in effect become stale, needs to be stressed. The absence of complaints also needs to be watched for; it will considerably weaken a claim of persistent misconduct if a string of appraisal reports on the employee's file make no reference to any problems. Full contemporaneous notes should be kept, in a form which will be understandable by a tribunal if subsequently called upon.

Taking a decision

One basic, but sometimes uncomfortable, idea is that it should be those conducting the meeting who determine its outcome. They are not therefore conducting a fact-finding exercise for the purpose of reporting to others who will take the necessary decisions. Thus, in the context of a grievance meeting, they will decide whether the grievance is justified and, if so, what the appropriate response should be. Equally, in the case of a disciplinary hearing, they need to consider whether the complaint about the employee is made out and, if so, what consequential decision, e.g. reprimand/warning/dismissal is appropriate and proportional.

Implementing the decision

The decision should be taken either at the end of the meeting, or as soon as possible after that, and should then be promptly communicated to the employee, and confirmed in writing. The procedures should provide for a right of appeal against any adverse finding, and the employee should have those rights confirmed to him, with details of how to proceed if he so wishes. Records of all decisions should be carefully kept on the employee's file. If the outcome is a warning, the time period during which it will be regarded as effective should be stated, as should the means by which the parties can recognise and measure any improvement in performance.

Notes

1   Belbin, R.M. (1981) *Management Teams: Why they succeed or fail*, Butterworth Heinemann and (1993) *Team Roles at Work*, Butterworth Heinemann.
2   This can be downloaded from **www.acas.org.uk/publications/pdf/CP01.pdf.**

7

Accounts and finance

This chapter examines the central role played by the accounting and financial data available to a firm and its partners. It seeks to show how a fear of accounts can be overcome by learning to concentrate on the essentials, and how an understanding of the key points will help the new partner to assess the health of the business he is joining. Key performance indicators are examined, so that consistent analysis can be achieved, and issues which bear upon the partnership agreement may be identified. Methods of assessing the profitability of the firm and its departments are considered and, finally, ways in which the firm's performance can be 'benchmarked' against that of its peers are offered.

General

Introduction

Many lawyers are, quite simply, frightened of accounts. In many ways this is surprising, since there are so many occasions in casework terms when a knowledge of accounts is needed, whether it be by a commercial lawyer perusing a client's accounts on a takeover, or a personal injury lawyer assessing the special damages suffered by his self-employed client. The problem may be, in part, the result of the fact that in these situations reliance is often placed upon external accounting expertise. In order to evaluate the firm before joining it, and in order to perform his tasks as a partner once admitted to the firm, it is essential that any prospective partner fully understands the accounting position of the firm.

Sources of detailed help

This chapter will indicate ways in which new partners can learn to mitigate the problems highlighted, but there will be circumstances in which a more detailed examination will be needed. In many instances, the help required can be obtained from works by Andrew Otterburn,[1] or Stephen Mayson.[2]

Selecting information

In many ways, the key to reading any set of accounts is to know in advance what you are looking for. If there is a key indicator which you want to examine, it is easy to concentrate upon that. Later parts of this chapter will suggest a number of such indicators. If then you wish to see how that affects other matters, or vice versa, you can broaden the approach. By then you have established your starting point, rather than just staring at the page and wondering what it can tell you.

Taking a basic overview

For example, when assessing a firm which you are being invited to join, the question uppermost in your mind might be how much profit you as an equity partner would be likely to earn. When looking at the profit and loss account (P&L) you can therefore ignore turnover and expenditure levels, and (knowing the number of existing equity partners) go straight to the bottom line, net profit, and do a simple division. Having ascertained that, you might wish to know how the average figure you have just ascertained is distributed in practice. You can then go to the notes as to the partners' current accounts, where individual profit shares are set out. You might wish to discover how the profit, as a percentage of turnover (i.e. net profit) compares to that of other firms. Back to the P&L, find the net profit line again, and divide into the top line. Finally, you might wish to know the general capital position. The balance sheet will give you the excess of assets over liabilities, and the notes as to the partners' capital and current accounts will give the distribution of this excess between the partners. If a deficit is discovered, this will obviously be a very clear warning signal! An overview of the firm's overall position, and of how that impacts upon individual partners has been obtained by looking at five lines of figures and performing two simple calculations.

Accounts as trend indicators

Two of the drawbacks with conventional accounts is that they are static and historical. They either refer to a set period of time, e.g. a P&L covering one year; or are a snapshot at a particular moment of time, e.g. a balance sheet giving balances on the last day of the year, with no indication of how those balances may have fluctuated over the year. They are also entirely retrospective, i.e. they only tell what *has* happened, possibly many months ago, not what *is currently* happening. What will actually be required is usually information not only about the immediate position, but also some help in predicting future events. For these purposes, accounts information becomes useful as an indicator of trends. In such cases, the data needed is often more readily understood in graphical form, and those responsible for the presentation of figures to partners, e.g. a practice manager, should be encouraged to offer the appropriate figures in such a form.

The principle of benchmarking

Another way in which the absolute figures produced by accounts may be lacking in real meaning is that there is no illustration of their comparison with other business units. What the reader may well want to know is how one firm compares with the industry norms. This process is called 'benchmarking', and is referred to in more detail later in this chapter. The practice of benchmarking should, however, be approached with caution, so as to ensure that like is really compared with like. The database from which any data used for benchmarking is taken thus needs to be carefully considered.

Access to the firm's accounts

Historically, many firms would invite potential new partners to join, either as full equity partners or often, as an interim measure, as salaried partners, without ever offering to show them the accounts. Amazingly, some (even amongst the largest firms) still do this. If an offer is made to any potential new partner on those terms, the best advice is simply, if politely, to decline and walk away.

If the partners wish an incoming partner to join them in accepting liability to third parties for the firm's debts, they should be prepared to accept that the least he will need to do is to check the current financial health of the firm. Bear in mind that in terms of a claim issued by a third party, there is no difference in concept between equity and salaried partners. Further, since the newcomer may not be an expert in accounts, the existing partners should be prepared for him to take, at his own cost, independent professional advice upon the accounts. It may, however, be reasonable for them to require that this advice is not sought from certain firms, where it might be felt to have some commercial sensitivity.

Key indicators for assessment

Suggested indicators

This part of the chapter offers a suggestion of seven potentially key indicators of a firm's financial position. If an incoming partner can get to grips with these, he will be well placed to consider whether or not to proceed. Furthermore, if he does go ahead, he will have a good grasp of the overall financial dynamics of the firm, to serve as an information base for his future involvement. The indicators suggested are:

- net profit per equity partner;
- turnover levels;
- the cash position;
- working capital requirements;
- the investment of partners' funds;
- work in progress; and
- lock up.

Net profit per equity partner

If the basic raison d'être of a firm is to make profit for those who own it, the first key measure which shows the health of the firm is not net profit, but rather net profit per equity partner. To illustrate the difference, consider a firm which in three successive years makes profit of £400,000, £450,000 and £480,000. That might be thought to indicate a reasonable trend in the firm's fortunes. If however the information is added that the firm had four partners in the first year, five in the second and six in the third, a different pattern emerges, as set out in Figure 7.1 below.

Therefore, when looking at the performance of any firm, it is important to consider the number of equity partners (which should always be indicated in the accounts) as well as the ostensible profit performance. The theme of the consideration of profitability is developed further later in this chapter.

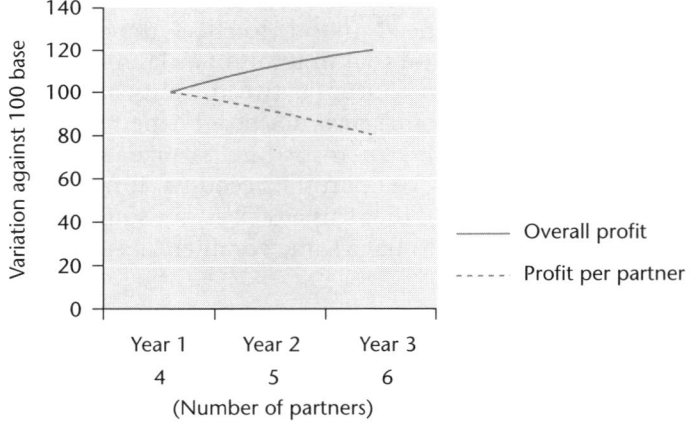

Figure 7.1 Illustration of difference between total profit and net profit per partner.

Turnover

Turnover (used in this context simply as total fees billed) is again apparently an absolute, but it is often more useful when viewed as an indicator of trends, broken down into constituent parts, or related to expenditure or profit to produce trackable ratios. As a statement on its own, turnover means little; if an outsider is told that a firm has a turnover of £5 million, that can mean little to him. Only if he knows: what expenditure is needed to generate that income, and hence what profit is achieved; how many people it took to produce the work; how many people will receive the resultant profit; and what change there has been in recent years in arriving at that figure, will he start to get a realistic picture of the firm.

Turnover as a trend

An indicator of immediate interest is therefore any change in turnover over the last two or three years. Any firm may, for particular reasons, either internal or external, have a year which was not as good as its predecessor. However, unless overall patterns show a business unit which has a steady year-on-year growth, after allowing for inflation, then the natural reaction will be concern for the firm's future viability. One word of warning however, when considering this or any other trend in the firm's financial statistics, is to ensure that there are no changes in accounting policy which might have resulted in hidden changes in the ostensible performance. For instance, when considering turnover, a check needs to be made that there has not been any change in policy in turning work in progress into bills, e.g. a new and more aggressive interim billing approach, which will tend to inflate turnover over a short period, or moving from rendering an invoice when the task is completed to when it is paid for, which will have the opposite effect. In both scenarios, the work being done, and the money being paid for it, are exactly the same as if there were no policy change at all, but the point in time at which the resultant figures enter the accounting data may be radically different. Information regarding operational policies such as these will probably not appear on the accounts themselves so, if an incoming partner is not aware of any such changes, he should make enquiries of the firm's accounts office.

The importance of cash

Work in progress is good, turnover is better, profit is best, but cash is king. Work in progress may not become turnover if bills are not fully and promptly rendered. Turnover may not become profit if expenditure goes up. Profit may not become cash if bills are not paid. In the end, it is cash that counts, as only cash can be used to pay the bills and to reward the partners. It seems almost trite to set matters out so simplistically, but the fact remains that it is not always appreciated that the rules are this simple, and that more businesses face insolvency because of overtrading, i.e. concentrating on obtaining and performing work without having either the resources to do the work efficiently or an effective system for billing and collecting fees, than ever suffer from too little on the order book.

The volatility of cash

The problem, from the point of view of examining accounts, is that cash is by far the most volatile factor, and is not clearly illustrated in conventional accounts. All that the accounts will indicate is the snapshot figure of the overall bank balances on one day in the year, i.e. that of the balance sheet. Cash can vary hugely from day to day. The firm's bank accounts will look very different on the day after the payment of the salaries for the month, the quarter's rent and the VAT cheque. So, again, some questions need to be asked. All firms should produce cashflow forecasts, not as a matter of law, but as a matter of compliance with any systematic management standards that they have adopted (e.g. Lexcel, etc. – see Chapter 3) or, at least, as a matter of prudence. They should also produce regular (monthly or quarterly) analyses of variation against the cashflow forecast. A prospective partner should always ask to see these documents.

Cashflow forecasts

The forecast should show whether, once all payments which can be predicted during the year are made, the cash position can be expected to improve. Note that in this sense 'payments' is much wider than the items which will appear under 'Expenditure' in the P&L, since it will include items such as: capital expenditure (e.g. a one-off payment for a computer system); payments of the VAT collected on behalf of HM Customs & Excise; and payments to or on behalf of the partners (e.g. drawings by them and income tax paid on their behalf). The analysis of variances against forecast should show whether predictions are being borne out by the actual performance of the firm. If the variance is negative, the prospective partner should ask for some explanation of why that is so and seek some reassurance as to how the situation is to be redressed. He should also discover how, if the business trades with the benefit of external finance, the position is viewed by those parties who are interested (the bank, leasing finance providers, etc.).

Working capital

Definitions and sources

The term 'working capital' is fairly loosely used. Technically, its definition is the excess of the firm's current assets over its current liabilities. Otherwise, it is used to refer to the provision of the finance needed for the day-to-day operations of the business, i.e. the aggregate of work in progress, unpaid bills and unrecovered disbursements. It can, in effect, be funded by one of two ways, i.e. the internal provision of funds by partners (whether via specifically introduced capital or retained profit) or external sources (such as, most typically, bank debt).

Adequate levels of working capital

A commonly-raised question is what the level of working capital should be. There is no simple answer, but the general view is that there should be enough working capital, i.e. enough cash available, to meet the expenditure needs of the firm for the next three to six months. Since those needs will fluctuate as expenditure fluctuates, it follows that a prudent working capital figure will also fluctuate. For peace of mind, it is always better to overestimate.

Partners' funds

The concept of partners' funds

Working capital is therefore one element in the process of answering two other commonly-asked questions, namely how much should the level of investment of partners' funds be, and how (if the firm has borrowings) should they compare with the level of external funding. The term 'partners' funds', rather than 'capital' has been used here, as different firms treat such funds, for internal accounting purposes, in different ways. They may, for instance, call everything a 'capital account'. They may, at another extreme, show separately 'capital' accounts, 'current' accounts, and 'loan' accounts. Such separations are for purely internal reasons; and the reality is that they all, in the aggregate, represent monies which, in one way or another, the partners have put into, or have allowed to remain in, the firm, but which they expect one day to take out. 'Partners' funds' is therefore a blanket term for all monies thus contributed by partners.

The need for investment by partners

As to the correct overall level of such funds, again there is no simplistic answer. It is a balancing exercise. On the one hand there is the question of how much the firm needs, not only in terms of working capital, but also for longterm investment purposes. Often the largest single item is the property from which the partnership practises. If this is beneficially owned by the partnership, then that will reflect in the capital figures. Likewise, if there has been extensive expenditure to fit out a leasehold property. Coming up fast on the rails, as the next largest item of capital commitment, is IT expenditure, as the investment requirements continue to climb.

Drawbacks of over-providing partners' funds

On the other, there are powerful disincentives for too much partner investment. First, it will be discouraging if partners year on year see that they are in theory making substantial profits, but they are unable to realise those profits in take-home terms, because the business is facing continual demands for further investment, and the profits are needed for that purpose. Second, if overall capital levels are high, potential new entrants to the partnership will be faced with either having to take out substantial personal loans to fund their capital contributions or (if deferment of input is allowed by the firm) they will be required to mortgage their profit share for years to come in order to allow a sufficient proportion of it to be retained in the firm so to build up their balance. Furthermore, looking at the opposite end of the spectrum, high capital levels can make it very difficult to finance the payment of capital to retiring partners. If firms have a number of partners who are close in age (not uncommon where a group of contemporaries have founded or expanded a firm together), the prospect of the grouping effect of retirements can present a very daunting picture to incoming partners.

Balancing internal and external funding

As to the acceptable relative levels of internal and external investment, again there are no certainties. For partners, there is the balance between wanting to borrow funds, to minimise their own initial contributions and to withdraw the maximum proportion of their subsequent profits; and the realisation that all such borrowings will need to be financed and, some day, paid back. From a banker's perspective, there is the balance between the fact that banks exist to lend monies, and make their profits from so doing, and not wanting to risk funds in a business enterprise where the entrepreneurs themselves do not show their personal faith in its viability by investing their own funds.

Return on investment/capital

Another way of looking at capital levels is that of the 'return on investment' or 'return on capital', often abbreviated as 'ROI' or 'ROC'. These are alternative terms for an attempt to measure the productivity of capital itself, to be able to compare it with different firms, different industries, or even different ways of investing money. At its simplest, if £100,000 is invested in an account with a fluctuating interest rate, but over a year has a total interest yield of £5,000, then it has an ROI rating of five per cent.

Unfortunately, it is not possible to treat a partner's investment in a firm in the same way, since his return (profit share) will derive not only from the use of his capital, but also from his personal fee-earning and managerial input, i.e. the capital is creating for him the opportunity to use his expertise and time to profitable effect. Even if, therefore, the firm's profit-sharing arrangements are constructed to provide for the payment of interest on capital as a first charge on profits, the resultant figure will only show part (and a notional part at that) of the true ROI figure. Use of ROI should therefore be treated with caution.

Work in progress

Introduction

The issue of work in progress ('WIP') has caused much trouble in recent years, particularly as a result of a change in the ways in which it is considered for tax purposes. This may make comparisons of accounts over a number of recent years quite difficult. It has, however, assumed greater importance than before, and so it is worth considering in the process of researching a firm's true position.

Work in progress as a cost

WIP is a cost. It is the expense to the firm of producing an asset, i.e. work, which has not yet been sold. Its industrial counterpart is the cost of acquiring and working on an asset, i.e. goods, which are to be sold. The difference is that in the context of a professional service business such as a law firm, there is no initial acquisition cost of the asset, merely the cost of the work itself. Hopefully, in both scenarios, the asset created will be sold for more than its cost, but that may not be the case. There may be no market for the goods, or the work done may not be fully recoverable, e.g. because the cost of the work in a fixed-fee matter exceeds the amount which can actually be charged. The principle of valuation to be adopted for tax purposes is therefore the same in both an industrial and a professional service context, i.e. it is the lesser of the actual cost and the realisable value.

Partners' work in progress

One curiosity of this approach is with regard to the work being undertaken by equity partners themselves. Since they are in the dual position of producers of work, and owners of the business, it is taken that their own work has no time cost attached to it, since they are not paying themselves to do it.[3] For this reason, the WIP which now has to appear in the accounts, ostensibly in full, will always be a considerable understatement of the billing potential of the firm, as it completely ignores the partners' own productivity. Hopefully, for the suitably inquisitive prospective partner, this gap in the firm's data can be remedied by looking at the firm's management accounts, which are likely to include partners' aggregated time costs. However, check that these are shown at cost and not at billing price, or the comparison with non-partners' figures in the accounts themselves will be distorted. New partners should also be astute to see how this issue is handled in the partnership agreement for outgoing partners, i.e. are they paid any element of WIP over and above their entitlement as indicated by the accounts, and, if so, how is that calculated?

The appearance of work in progress in accounts

WIP features in the accounts in two ways. First, because it is an asset of the firm, it is shown as such in the balance sheet, as an absolute figure. At the end of the year, therefore, it is the joint task of the firm's accounts managers, and the external accountants, to get together and agree the level for the year. Second, the year-on-year change in the figure, because it is held by the Inland Revenue to represent a change in the potential income level of the firm, is shown as a plus or minus figure in the income section of the P&L, depending on whether the WIP level has increased or decreased. Thus tax is payable on the movement in the WIP figure.

Calculating work in progress

Historically, WIP was of relatively little importance for law firms. Some firms, trading on the 'cash basis' (i.e. where they did not count invoices for accounting purposes until they were paid by clients) did not even include WIP in their accounts at all. Others might have had some archaic formula, e.g. a percentage of overheads, which had been agreed with the Inland Revenue back in the mists of time. Yet others gave some approximation of what they believed the real figure to be. So long as the method of calculation of WIP was consistent, it was assumed that the Inland Revenue would get its tax in the end, when the billing and payment process was complete. In 1999, however, all that changed.[4]

The new regime

The Inland Revenue had come to the view that it was in fact losing out because firms were not fully valuing their WIP, and hence were effectively deferring the tax payable in respect of it, without having to pay any interest. It therefore determined to require all firms, whatever their historical treatment, to bring WIP into their accounts at its full value for the first accounting period commencing after 6 April 1999. It was however recognised that to do so would mean a potentially vast change for some firms. Firms with little or no WIP, would suddenly have to show several months' worth of potential billing as taxable income, and would have a major tax payment to make, without any change in the actual cash receipts available to fund such a payment. Provision was therefore made for a 'catch-up' charge for this one-off increase, payable over 10 years, and payable by those persons who are equity partners in each of those 10 years, according to their then applicable profit-sharing ratios.

Adjusting to the changes

These changes have created a number of problems, and opportunities as well. The magnitude will depend on the difference between the results of the new treatment and the old, i.e. they are likely to be greatest for those firms which previously used the cash basis. The first problem is that, in reality, 10 years is far too long a period to represent the time at which the WIP will be released, i.e. turned into billing and paid for. Therefore those equity partners who join the firm towards the latter part of the 10-year period will be paying tax on a figure which has no bearing on monies actually receivable by them. They may therefore want to see some provision in the partnership agreement to adjust for this. The second point, which is a mixed blessing, is that the figure for WIP on the balance sheet is likely to increase significantly. The advantage of this is that, for the first time, what is a very real asset of the firm will appear in its accounts. No longer will bank managers and other providers of funds need to be reassured that there is value on the firm's future, even though little of it is shown in the accounts. They may however still need to be reminded that, as above, partners' WIP is still not shown, so there is still a significant element of undervaluation.

Owning the work in progress

A straightforward approach

The possibly difficult counterpart to this, however, is working out who owns this suddenly created capital asset, bearing in mind that whoever owns the asset will, one day, wish to be paid for it. The straightforward way of dealing with the matter is to consider the uplift in WIP to be a capital profit, to be divided between the equity partners for the year in which it appears in the profit-sharing ratios applicable to that year, and for it to be consequently credited to those partners' capital accounts.

A more complex approach

A counter-argument however runs along the lines that this is a mythical figure, created purely as a result in bookkeeping changes, with no actual cash consequences. Therefore if it is credited to partners' capital accounts, those who retire first from the firm will benefit at the expense of those who remain, since the former will expect the latter to pay them hard cash for the intangible asset. The proponents of this argument therefore contend that the uplift in WIP should be transferred to an unattributed revaluation reserve account, and not allocated to any partner for so long as the firm continues. This, they suggest, fits with the cultural concept that partners at any given time are to an extent custodians of the partnership for future generations. Against that, the more senior partners are likely to advocate the view that the reality is that the uplift in WIP represents work which was actually done – and, being a cost, paid for – during the period when they were the partners, and thus it is right that they in the long term should benefit from it. Creating this reserve would effectively defer a decision as to who should benefit in personal terms until the happening of an event which might bring the firm's existence as a separately identifiable body to an end (i.e. perhaps merger, or definitely dissolution). It almost becomes a test of endurance to see who lasts longest, or a tontine. Incidentally, transfer of the firm's business into a limited liability partnership would not need to be an event of this nature.

Lock up

At first sight, high levels of WIP might seem to be desirable. After all, it shows now in the balance sheet as an asset, and represents an entitlement to future earnings. Anecdotes abound of senior partners who have regarded filing cabinets full of unbilled files as capital reserves. Although there is an element of truth in showing the true value of WIP as an asset, the whole truth is somewhat different. WIP is in fact one of the two elements which together make up the 'lock up' of a firm, the other being debtors. Between them, what they represent is the gap in time – and hence cost – between the partners paying for work to be done on a client's behalf, and being paid by that client for that job. Looked at simplistically, if there were no gap at all, the partners would be able to pay each month's wages and overheads from that month's receipts, which would represent that month's work. In reality, since there always will be a gap before work is paid for, in the interim the partners must fund the continuing payment of wages and overheads, either by provision of their own funds, or by borrowing. If their own funds are used, there is an indirect opportunity cost, since the monies are not available for investment elsewhere; and if there are borrowings, there is the direct cost of the interest. Ultimately, of course, if the gap between carrying out the work and receiving payment widens too far, the firm may not be able to find the money from any source to continue to fund expenditure, and difficulties or even insolvency may result.

Measuring these concepts in days

All of these three concepts, WIP, debtors and lock up, are commonly measured in terms of days, i.e. as a proportion of the firm's overall income. If, for example, a firm had a turnover of £1,200,000, WIP of £200,000, and debtors of £300,000, then it would be considered to have:

- 60 days' WIP;
- 90 days' debtors; and
- 150 days' lock up.

The question of what represents an acceptable level of lock up will be returned to when benchmarking is considered. The simplest ways of reducing the levels will be, on the one hand, prompt billing and interim billing and, on the other, better credit control procedures for those clients who are slow in paying bills.

Profitability

Profitability at the firm level

The measures of profit in absolute terms at the level of the firm (that is as distinct from any department or individual within the firm) were looked at above. What is often as helpful, however, particularly when examining trends or benchmarking the firm's performance, is to look at profit ratios, i.e. the proportion of the firm's turnover which ends up being distributable to the partners as profit. Since this is relative to the firm overall, it is not expressed in 'per partner' terms.

The difficulties of measurement

There may however be different elements to take into consideration, and it is always important to know which ratio is being used, especially when considering the position over a period of years, or between different firms. For instance, if a firm has fee income of £1,000,000 and distributable operating profit of £250,000, it has a net profit ratio of 25 per cent. Assume that, in addition to its fee income, it has a surplus of interest earned on client funds over interest paid to clients of £100,000. It then has total income of £1,100,000 and distributable funds of £350,000, i.e. a ratio of 31.8 per cent. If comparing that year's performance with another year for the same firm, is the right comparator 25 per cent, since that represents the firm's operational performance, or 31.8 per cent which includes at least partly a factor which is outside the control of the firm, i.e. fluctuating interest rates? Alternatively, if comparing against another firm, was their ratio calculated by including or excluding their interest yield? One more thing to remember when assessing profit is that it is possible to inflate profit artificially for a short period by failure to invest. Thus if a firm's profit figures appear high, the question still has to be asked as to how they are providing for the future in terms of, e.g. recruiting and training staff, acquiring up-to-date IT equipment, etc.

Profitability at departmental level

The departmental picture of profitability may be totally different from that at the overall firm level. If, for instance, the firm in the above example has two departments, the first of which yields £600,000 and costs £400,000, and the second yields £400,000 and costs £350,000, then their respective profit ratios are 33.3 per cent and 12.5 per cent. Thus the overall figure can hide major disparities, and it is important for the firm's management to be aware of this.

Attributing departmental costs

The difficulty is working out what is the cost of each department's output. Some items may be easy to attribute directly. For instance, the salary and national insurance cost of a fee earner who works exclusively within one department and has no management function, can only be regarded as a direct cost of the department within which he works. Other costs will have to be apportioned if they are to be included within the calculation, e.g. the employment costs of a telephonist who handles calls for all departments. There may be relatively accurate ways of apportioning the cost, e.g. if the firm's call-logging software is sophisticated enough for this to be done by reference to the number of calls handled for each department. Alternatively, there may be a need for some rough-and-ready method such as allocating cost according to the proportions of the departments' turnover, on the basis that these reflect activity levels and therefore cost implications.

Notional salaries for partners

Another variable which needs to be considered is the work carried out by partners themselves. Their input is not, of course, a cost, and so does not show in the normal accounting data. It can however reflect major differences in the reality of the situation. For instance, going back to the example above, if there are four partners working in the first department, but only one in the second, the apparent disparity vanishes, since in each case the department is yielding a net £50,000 per partner. One way of accounting for this is therefore to include, as an extra cost, a notional salary per partner. If this is done, however, care needs to be taken when using the resultant data, which should not be compared back to other figures without making any adjustment necessary. For instance, if trying to relate it back to the firm's profitability figures, the notional salary levels would have to be discounted fully. If making a comparison with data from another firm, the question would need to be asked as to what notional salary assumptions had been made there, and what should be done to make the two sets of figures directly comparable.

Approaches to departmental analysis

A straightforward approach

There are different approaches to how much detail it is useful to include when producing departmental figures. One approach is that, if the object of the exercise is simply to compare different areas of a firm's practice, the turnover, which is easily ascertainable from an analysis of bills rendered, can be divided by the direct staff costs of those working within the department, allowing for partners' notional salaries if desired. All other expenses, e.g. salaries, etc. for those whose work cannot be neatly pigeonholed such as administrative staff, and all overheads such as property and marketing costs, are ignored.

A more complex approach

The other extreme is to say that all costs have to be allocated somewhere within the matrix, and that if they cannot be directly attributed they must be apportioned somehow. Thus if, in the example above, using an apportionment as to turnover, the firm had spent £120,000 on a computer system, comprising £20,000 of specialist software for the first department only, and £100,000 of general hardware and software for the benefit of all fee-earning and administrative staff, then the first £20,000 would be attributed directly to the first department, and the balance would be attributed as to £60,000 to the first and £40,000 to the second. This can become a very complex exercise, and involve many assumptions. For instance, if the managing partner spends half his time as a fee earner in the first department, and the other half on the management of the firm, is his notional salary attributed totally to the first department, or is only half so attributed, with the other half being apportioned as above? And what of his secretary's costs?

Consistency of analytical technique

It is easy for the detail to overtake the benefits, and for hours to be spent compiling figures (bearing in mind that the various assumed figures will not appear in the firm's standard accounting data, so that calculations will need to be done either manually or by carrying out complex spreadsheet exercises) to which little attention may eventually be paid. The key is to start with a system which is acknowledged as being fair, and then stick to that. It is the comparatives and trends indicated by these figures which are likely to be significant, not the figures as absolutes, since too many assumptions have been required to allow them to be used for anything other than a broad-brush approach. What counts therefore is consistency of compilation.

Profitability at individual level

The same problems in undertaking departmental analysis will affect any attempt to arrive at a figure for the profitability of an individual fee earner. Again, it is of course (assuming he has no managerial responsibilities) relatively easy to attribute to him the direct costs of his production, i.e. his own salary and national insurance costs, and those of anyone working directly for him, e.g. his secretary. Comparing this against his personal billing will produce a profitability ratio for him. If, however, one tries to apportion overheads to him, the problems begin. Generally, it will be sufficient to stay at the basic level of analysis, since what will be looked for is his performance against a given norm. There will also be other metrics which can readily be assessed in regard to the fee earner, e.g. chargeable hours recorded, billing records, recovery, etc.

Benchmarking

The principles of benchmarking

Benchmarking is simply an exercise to enable partners to test various aspects of their firm's performance against that of their counterparts and peers. The exercise may highlight areas of under performance and the reasons for these. Equally, it may reveal that the firm has outperformed other comparable firms. Benchmarking has been commonly used for financial performance, since the wealth of statistics which financial analysis offers gives rise to ready comparison, but increasingly the technique is being extended into other areas, such as human resources policies, IT strategies, etc.

Available data for benchmarking

In the early days of benchmarking, it was mostly undertaken on behalf of firms as a commercial exercise, by such organisations as the Centre for Inter-Firm Comparison, who market their product under the name 'Paragon'. A number of firms still participate in this programme, and a prospective partner would do well to try to obtain the information they provide. Naturally, only participating and paying firms get the full report, but extracts are used for publicity purposes by the Centre, and may give some generally useful information. In recent years, an annual benchmarking survey has been undertaken on behalf of *The Lawyer* by PricewaterhouseCoopers,[5] which is both comprehensive and detailed. More recently, the Law Management Section of the Law Society (LMS) has arranged a survey of volunteer firms from amongst its membership, carried out by BDO Stoy Hayward.[6] Some local law societies arrange for their own surveys to be conducted, usually by firms of accountants. Their results are normally only made available to members, but are particularly useful since they reflect local experience.

Cautions applicable to benchmarking data

A number of factors need to be taken into account, however, when using any benchmarking data. These include:

- *Time*. The first thing to be careful about is the time to which the data relate. It is of no use to set your firm's performance against a benchmark average if it relates to accounts prepared two or three years ago, as market conditions will inevitably have moved on since then. This is perhaps less of a worry with ratios than absolute figures (i.e. there may still be more validity in knowing average profit ratios than absolute profit per partner figures) but even there the more contemporaneous the sample the better.
- *Size of firm*. The next is that the figures will mean much more if they are for firms of a comparable profile. For instance, it is not much use for a sole practitioner in a provincial High Street firm to know the performance ratios of a 'Magic Circle' firm. Users of the comparisons need to know how they are performing against their peers, i.e. firms of the same size and in the same area. Some surveys, e.g. those from PWC, take considerable pains to break down their data this way.
- *Type of work*. One aspect of comparative profiling is the nature of work undertaken by the firms. Two next-door firms could be of similar size in terms of numbers of partners, but if one is doing publicly funded crime, family and immigration work, and the other is conducting mergers and acquisitions work for the largest local companies, they may learn little from each other. Unfortunately, it is

almost impossible to eliminate this element from any sampling, which in turn means that the size of the sample becomes more important, so that the statistically distorting effect of firms at the polarised ends of any scale will be minimised.

- *Selection of analysed firms.* Another difficulty is in the method of selection of the firms. Some surveys will be by invitation, e.g. local law societies' surveys of firms in one area, or the LMS survey of its member firms. Others will come from requests to participate made to preselected groups, e.g. the survey by PWC which is given a list by *The Lawyer* of the 'top' firms to contact.[7] In any event, there will then be an element of self-selection, since of course not all firms will respond to such requests.

- *Accounting methodology.* One of the reasons firms may not participate in a survey reflects a further difficulty with benchmarking, which is ensuring that like is compared with like so far as is possible. The problem is that firms may, perfectly legitimately and for good internal reasons, prepare their accounts in totally different ways. The task of those undertaking the survey is to try to strip out those differences to get at the underlying facts. Certain firms will not want to commit to the time it takes to adjust their accounts figures to the required format, and so will not participate. A simple example will suffice. Firm A shows net profit per partner of £90,000; firm B £95,000. Firm A provides its partners with cars costing £30,000 each, and pays all private and business motoring expenses. Firm B relies on its partners to provide their own cars, and merely pays a flat rate per mile for business usage. Who is better off – a partner in firm A or one in firm B?

Notes

1   Otterburn, A. (2002) *Profitability and Law Firm Management*, Law Society.
2   Mayson, S. (1997) *Making Sense of Law Firms*, Blackstone Press.
3   This is not the case for limited liability partnerships. The Statement of Recommended Practice issued by the Consultative Committee of Accountancy Bodies in May 2002 indicates that the 'overhead element' of members' work in progress does need to be brought into account. The one-off cost of bringing this in on conversion to LLP status may prove a disincentive to conversion for some firms.
4   Finance Act 1998, s.44, Sched. 6, as amplified by Standard Statement of Accounting Practice 9 (issued by the Institute of Chartered Accountants in England and Wales).
5   Copies of the report can be obtained from PricewaterhouseCoopers at the cost of £150 (2003). See **http://www.pwcglobal.com/extweb/SendMail Substitute.nsf/UK_Law_ Survey?OpenForm#exec.**

6   Copies of the report can be obtained from the LMS at a small fee
     (**http://www.lms.lawsociety.org.uk**) or see Andrew Otterburn (**note 1** above)
     which uses the 2001 data.
7   When the author enquired of the collator of the PWC survey what criteria
     were used by *The Lawyer* to ascertain what made a firm a 'top' one, she did
     not know the answer!

8

Treatment of profits

This chapter considers the ways in which partners may be
remunerated. It contrasts this with their previous remuneration as
employees, and then examines the various approaches to the
calculation of an individual's profit entitlement. It links these matters
to the partner's investment in the business, the attainment of the
firm's strategy and the culture of the firm.

General

Introduction

There are various motives for seeking partnership, but undoubtedly a
major factor will be the desire to increase remuneration, which in turn
depends on the assumption that the firm will yield sufficient profits to
pay its partners more than it does its staff. The new partner may often
assume that the wisdom of the senior partners has produced a fair and
equitable profit-sharing system, or he may accept that any current system
will not be changeable. Few incoming partners will have any real immediate choice in the remuneration method to be adopted, and few will
therefore stop to consider whether the profit-sharing structure may in
fact be an obstacle to the firm's attainment of its stated aims. There is a
huge variety of methods available – so much so that there is no real
'norm' applicable as a universal starting point.

Joining the firm

Prior to joining the practice, most incoming partners will have had the
greater part of their remuneration paid in terms of straightforward salary,
subject to PAYE and employee's NIC. They may also have enjoyed some
form of bonus scheme, linked perhaps to turnover for themselves, their
department, or the firm as a whole. They will probably also have received
some benefits in kind. Again, through the mechanism of the PAYE
scheme, and by delivery of the tax form P11D in respect of their annual
benefits, they will have paid tax on any such bonuses and benefits.

Generally, salary will have been paid towards the end of the month, in arrears. Once they become partners, all this will change.

Drawings

The pattern of drawings

For a start, the new partner will need to know whether there is any pattern to drawings. In the past, some firms, particularly the smallest ones, effectively allowed drawings on office account ad lib, relying merely on partners' good sense not to overdraw! An incoming partner should beware the obvious danger of abuse of such a system. Almost invariably, firms will allow monthly, or possibly quarterly drawings. This may, like salary, be in arrears, or it may be in advance at the start of the month. In any event, the new partner needs, for his own budgeting purposes, to know what and when he will be receiving on a regular basis.

Tax payments

The position before self-assessment

A new partner also needs to know at the outset how partners' tax is, in practice, paid. It used to be the case that the partnership was responsible for the payment of individual partners' tax, insofar as it resulted from their share of the partnership profits. Since partners were jointly liable for their partners' tax, it was natural that they wanted to ensure that funds were reserved to pay it. Thus drawings levels would be set so as to ensure that sufficient cash was available for retention within the firm, and the firm would in due course make the necessary payment to the Inland Revenue.

Self-assessment and the present position

In 1999[1] all of that changed. When the self-assessment scheme came in for Schedule D earners, such as partners, the joint liability for partners' tax ceased. There is no longer any legal reason why the partnership needs to retain funds for tax payments, and it is quite at liberty to assume that each partner will settle his own tax bills, on 31 January and 31 July each year. If that practice is adopted, it logically follows that the drawings level will be set to make payment on a gross basis, so that the individual can set aside sufficient monies in anticipation of his eventual tax liability.

Reservation of tax monies by the firm

In practice, however, many firms have continued their old ways, reserving the monies for tax within the firm, paying drawings on a net basis, and settling individuals' tax liabilities from centrally held funds. Even though partners may not be directly liable for each other, there could be considerable harm done to the firm as a whole if, say, one partner failed to pay his tax and consequently became bankrupt. The threat of such a position is a classic incentive to fraud and of course the firm could suffer serious harm to its reputation. The practice of retaining central control is thus a form of risk management. If control is central, the new partner should bear in mind that, whatever the firm decides to do, the Inland Revenue will hold him personally liable for his tax liability. He should therefore check that all payments due to be made on his behalf are fully and promptly paid, lest he suffer penalty and/or interest claims. If not, he should ensure that he keeps a reserve for his own personal tax liability.

Payment of undrawn profits

In order to budget as far as possible (subject always to overall profit calculations) a partner will wish to know what in practice will happen to that share of his profits for the year which is neither drawn by him nor (if appropriate) reserved for tax. Will there, for instance, be any interim distributions, e.g. quarterly or half-yearly, in anticipation of the profit levels indicated by the management accounts? Or will the firm be prudent, and wait until the annual profits have been established, either by the management accounts or the accountants' later figures, before allowing a retrospective withdrawal of undrawn profit?

Retention of profits by the firm

More fundamental still, the partner will need to know whether he will be able to take the undrawn profit at all, or whether the firm will expect him to leave this money in the firm. This may be either as a planned boost to his capital within the firm, or for a specific project that the partnership wants to fund internally, such as a major IT acquisition, or because it is required for working capital (which translates as the firm not having the cash to pay out partners' full earnings – whatever the theoretical profit level – without recourse to external borrowing which it either does not want to seek or is unable to obtain). Asking questions on these issues may not be comfortable, but the answers will serve not only to allow the partner to plan personal spending levels, but also to discover some fundamental truths about the anticipated cashflow position of the firm, and the extent to which, in addition to any contributions of capital, he will actually be asked to invest.

Salaried and fixed share partners

'Salaried' or 'fixed share' partnerships

It may be that, in an attempt to allow a transitional phase, a newcomer may be treated as either a salaried partner, or a fixed share partner. The terms are however often rather loosely used, and in particular 'salaried' partners may either be truly salaried, or fixed share. Usually, though not exclusively, such arrangements are on an interim basis only, and are effectively a rite of passage which newcomers feel obliged to accept in order to attain their eventual goal of equity status.

The salaried partner's position

For current purposes, a salaried partner is someone who is held out to the public as a partner, with the ostensible authority to act as a partner and hence the risks of personal liability attaching to a partner, while actually still being an employee, paid under PAYE and with employer and employee NIC payments continuing. The disadvantages of this are obvious, particularly from the individual's perspective. Becoming liable for a firm's debts, and claims against the firm, without any real chance of (an immediate) share in its potential profits, is not a logically attractive position. Even an indemnity[2] given by the partners will, if all goes wrong, only be as useful as the assets of the partners make it, and will not avoid either the possibility of third party claims being made directly against the individual, or the chance that insolvent partners may not be able to meet their indemnity obligations.

The advantages of salaried partnerships

By creating salaried partnerships, the firm is effectively hedging its bets, pacifying aspirants with an apparent rise in status and boosting its ostensible size in the public's eye, but reserving the option to see how that individual performs in a senior role before giving up its right, as an employer, to dismiss the employee. There can, however, be advantages from the individual's viewpoint as well. On the one hand, there may be those who aspire to full equity partnership, but would nonetheless like to look more closely at the sharp end of the partnership first, particularly if, on entry to equity, they will be asked to contribute substantial capital and commit themselves to more onerous restrictive covenants and notice periods. On the other hand there are those who prefer this status on a long-term basis, who do not ever want equity status, and are prepared to accept the viability of the partners' indemnity as covering the risk incurred by being held out as partners.

The fixed share partner's position

A fixed share partner, by contrast, is genuinely an equity partner, and is subject to the Schedule D self-assessment regime, rather than to PAYE. The share of the profit to which he is entitled is pegged in advance, either as an absolute figure, or as a capped amount subject to abatement if profit levels do not yield certain thresholds. He may even be internally liable for losses, or may be entitled to an indemnity similar to that referred to above for salaried partners.

Considerations if moving to a limited liability partnership

These arrangements should also be considered in the light of the possible operation of a practice under the umbrella of a limited liability partnership (see Chapter 2). Three points are relevant. First, salaried memberships are viable, just as salaried partnerships are. Section 4(4) of the LLP Act states: 'A member of a limited liability partnership shall not be regarded for any purposes as employed by the limited liability partnership unless, if he and the other members were partners in a partnership, he would be regarded for that purpose as employed by the partnership.' In other words, the LLP is entitled to make just the same sort of arrangements as a partnership.[3] Second, taking into account the comments above as to indemnities, there are obvious advantages to an individual under a system which limits personal liability. Lastly, therefore, the comments made in Chapter 2, to the effect that if there is any prospect of conversion to LLP status in the near future, it is better to do so before a new member joins, apply just as much to salaried or fixed share partners. It is their positions in respect of third party liabilities which are relevant to the argument, and those are no different from ordinary partners/members.

Interest on capital

The concept of interest on capital

If interest on capital is to be paid by a firm, it is effectively a first charge on profits, and has to be calculated before the amount of residual profit is ascertained for distribution between the partners. It is entirely a matter for the firm as to whether such interest is payable at all and the decision to pay it is likely to be influenced by the degree of equality in other aspects of the firm's financial position. To take one extreme, if capital is held equally between the partners, drawings are equal monthly amounts, and the eventual profit distribution is equal, there is no point in paying interest on capital, since those payments will also be equal, and will simply diminish what would otherwise be payable as profits by equal shares.

Since there is (at present, at least) no difference in the tax treatment of interest and profits, there is no advantage in choosing to pay interest. If, on the other hand, partners have significantly different levels of capital investment within the firm and receive significantly different shares of profit then it can be viewed as fair to reward that investment by the payment of interest, as an incentive for monies to be left within the firm to provide working capital.

The base figure for interest calculations

There are many possible approaches to the calculation of this interest. The first task is to decide what element interest is payable on. Some firms regard 'capital' as being solely chunks of specifically introduced capital, e.g. those raised by external borrowing by individuals for investment in the firm. Other monies attributed to partners in the firm's accounts from retained profits are set out separately as 'current accounts'. Depending on drawing patterns, there may be arrangements for the transfer of surplus tranches into capital accounts. Some will also show loan accounts, perhaps (but not always) if specific arrangements have been made. It is suggested that the true position is that any money held within the firm, whatever its label, is the individual partner's investment in that firm, and that if interest is to be payable, then it should be on the entirety of that sum, unless other specific arrangements apply to any part of it (such as loans).

The date for assessment of investment levels

The second question is the point in time at which the amount of capital on which interest is payable is determined. No system will capture the true position perfectly, but a consistent choice should be applied. Probably the easiest figure to take is the opening balance, since this is the closing balance in the previous year's accounts. An alternative is to use the closing balance, which will entail a delay before the figure can be ascertained. However, this not only makes for a longer delay before figures can be ascertained, but also involves making certain assumptions, since closing figures will involve calculating profit shares, and these cannot be calculated until interest allocation is known. Trying to adjust the figures as the year progresses (save, perhaps, in respect of any abnormal sums introduced or withdrawn) would be difficult to administer, and would be unlikely to achieve much real benefit.

The rate of interest payable

The third factor in the calculation is, of course, the rate of interest to be payable. This could be a set rate in the partnership agreement but, if the intention is to compensate partners for the opportunity cost of investing in the firm, it seems unfair to ignore market interest fluctuations. If a variable rate is chosen, e.g. two per cent above the base rate of the firm's bankers, then again the point at which that rate is to be taken needs to be determined. This time, it is suggested that rather than fixing the rate at the start of the year, it should be fixed at the end, since that is the closest date to the actual payment. If the amount upon which interest is to be paid is the opening balance at the start of the year, it is possible to apply a rate which varies throughout the year with base rate changes. It would be tedious to make the calculation but it is by no means impossible. If the closing balance is used, calculating variance over the year is illogical.

Payment or accrual of interest

Finally, the decision has to be made whether the interest should actually be paid out to the partners, or whether it should be simply allowed to accrue to the credit of their current account. This may, of course, be dictated by the firm's cash position, unless funds are abundant or reserves for likely levels of interest have been made. If cash allows, however, it seems logical for the interest to be paid, less any interim payments on account of interest which may already have been made. If the calculation is based on opening balances, and the rate on the last day of the year, the calculation is extremely simple and payment could be made the next day. The reasons for this are twofold. First, if the firm is compensating the partners for interest foregone on other investments, it should be paid by the firm no less frequently than annually. Second, if interest is simply allowed to accrue it will be applicable to the higher balances, and will exacerbate the differences between the levels of partners' investments within the firm. This could eventually cause resentment and become divisive.

Remuneration structures

Equality

In conceptual terms, the starting point for any consideration of different approaches to the distribution of partnership profits is equality. This is enshrined in statute, in section 24(1) of the Partnership Act 1890. That presumption of equality is repeated in regulation 7(1) of the Limited Liability Partnerships Regulations 2001.[4] The philosophical underpinning is that 'equality is equity'. Those partnerships which still follow this pattern implicitly adopt as their view of partnership that:

- the level of seniority of any partner makes no difference;
- each partner is (or, at least, over a given period of time, will be) making the same contribution in terms of input; and
- the partnership draws its strength from its diversity of talent, so that differences in output (e.g. billing) can be ignored.

Application of equality

Equality would, for instance, be a typical pattern for a newly created partnership of peers, particularly if there was no inequality of initial contribution, not in terms of capital (which can be compensated for by payment of interest, as above), but in terms of an existing client base. One incidental advantage offered by equality is the opportunity to keep capital levels running in parallel, if initial capital inputs and subsequent drawings are equal and (if the partnership continues to pay partners' tax centrally) tax payments are equal. Thus at the time of each half-year's tax payment, each partner could draw the difference between his personal tax bill and the highest tax bill of all the partners. That preservation of capital equality would avoid any potentially divisive arguments later about the consequences of capital inequality. One potential drawback, however, is that it effectively sets the level of capital expected from any incoming partner, unless the whole basis of the partnership finances is to be altered. Care should therefore be taken that the level set will be practical for any potential new partners to achieve.

Lockstep

General

Another classic method of profit distribution is lockstep, i.e. progress, from the time of joining the firm, through a gradual and pre-arranged increase, to a plateau applicable for all partners of at least a pre-set level of seniority. Some general points on this are:

- *Entry level.* This should relate to the salary which the incoming partners were earning as employees. In other words, it may be necessary for there to be a minimum level set, by way of protection for new partners, even if in a particular year this is more than they would have got by the normal application of the points or percentages chosen. In such a situation, the consequence will be that other partners' shares are reduced from what would otherwise be their levels.
- *Relative differences.* The ratio between the lowest and highest profit share should to be considered. According to a study of the top 100 firms by *Legal Business* in 2001, the range was from multiples of 1.21 to 4.58, with the average 2.35. It is not difficult to appreciate that a

junior partner might feel some resentment if he knows that a senior partner earns nearly five times as much as he does.

- *Capital.* The third point is that to some extent the differential is intended to reflect the greater capital contribution which is likely to have been made by the more senior partners. Thus, if new partners are required to bring in initially a full amount of capital, then part of the rationale for lockstep, or at least for a substantial difference in levels within such a system, will diminish.
- *Time for progression.* The final general point is that consideration should be given to the period over which partners progress to parity. Commonly, this would be about three to five years, but in some firms this may be 10 or even 15 years, which may be daunting in an era of increased partner mobility.

The rationale

The thinking behind lockstep is that, although the basis of equality is fundamentally correct, it should be recognised that, in the early years of the partnership, individuals will still be growing into the role. Newcomers should therefore have the promise of gradual growth in their profit share in recognition of the increasing wisdom and experience they will bring to the tasks required of a partner. Implicitly, this acknowledges the fact that a partner's contribution to a firm cannot be valued in terms only of his technical legal expertise, but must include the whole spectrum of activities such as client development, departmental management, etc.

Pros and cons

Proponents of lockstep, and there are many even in the largest of firms, consider that it offers a straightforward and predictable career path; that it provides maximum income at a time when professional input across the board is greatest and personal needs are there to match; and that it avoids divisive arguments about performance levels. Opponents, however, contend that it penalises new entrants, whose contribution to the firm in output (i.e. billing) terms may be greatest, and thus may feel that their seniors are living off their efforts. A number of features need to be present for lockstep to be sufficiently attractive to overcome these objections. First, and perhaps somewhat paradoxically, it needs a belief that the system will remain in place within the firm for the foreseeable future, so that incoming partners can feel confident that there will be sufficient years for them to enjoy plateau-level earnings to make the initial sacrifice worthwhile. This may be extremely difficult to offer in a climate where mergers abound. Next, it depends on a culture which requires equality of commitment and input, and that can put matters right if any given individual is not pulling his weight. It will be more difficult for new partners to accept the system if the period from start to plateau level is too long, or the differential between those two levels is too great.

Modified lockstep – five types

Stephen Mayson[5] has identified five possible modifications to lockstep, as follows:

- *Pre-retirement reduction.* One option is that, in the period before retirement, partners should have a (usually moderate) level of reduction in their profit share to reflect that they are making a reduced contribution. However, this may work unfairly against those who continue to perform at high levels despite advancing years.
- *Bonus pool.* A small percentage of profits may be reserved (Mayson suggests not exceeding five per cent) as a reward for those partners making exceptional contributions. A number of difficulties arise as to issues of assessment and determination, which are in effect the same as those referred to in regard to performance-related payments (below). Provision should be made that the full amount need not be paid out, so if there is not sufficient reason for distributing it, it should accrue to the tranche of profits distributable in the normal way. It will only work if the effect of the modification is to reduce, not enhance, any inequality. Thus, if the plateau-level partners are amongst the highest performers anyway, there would be little point in an extra slice being paid out for performance, but if the young Turks are in fact the high performers the case for a larger slice is more easily made.
- *Super-plateau.* The creation of a level, beyond parity, to which the 'stars' of the firm may aspire. The drawback to this is that it presupposes consistent performance at exceptional levels, which in turn raises similar assessment and determination issues.
- *Variable progression rates.* Progression between different levels of lockstep may be made dependent upon attainment of certain goals, rather than simply the passage of time, so that individual partners might be either accelerated through the stages, or held back. Again, assessment and determination issues apply.
- *Banded lockstep.* A variation of the last method, whereby there is automatic progression through a number of points to a particular stage, but there is then consideration of whether the partner can progress to the next band. This would seem to require an abnormally long number of years for progression to parity.

Performance-related division

General

It may seem simplistic to say so, but the first, and in many ways the most difficult problem, when introducing any form of performance pay, is to determine what aspects of performance are to be measured or assessed as the basis for the division. As mentioned above, there is no 'norm' for approaching the problem. Essentially, in choosing the measure or package of measures to use, firms should recognise that what they are trying to do is reward a particular sort of behaviour or output, and that it therefore makes no sense to recognise factors which are not themselves inherently important to the firm's strategic plan. Thus, if the firm's plan is to achieve a set percentage of penetration into a particular market sector, which requires partners' skills to be concentrated towards marketing efforts so that fee earning is done at a delegated level, it will make little sense to reward partners for their own individual billings as this would encourage them to withhold their efforts from the planned marketing activities. On the other hand, if there are concerns that the firm is over-trading, i.e. it has taken on too much work for the resources available to it, so that partners' efforts are needed at the fee-earning coalface, it is illogical to reward them for extended client development projects.

Selecting a single measure

At first sight, the easiest way of approaching the problem is to choose a suitable, objectively measurable, factor, and to relate performance solely to that. The classic factor would be simple billing by individual partners (always the measure to which lawyers are immediately attracted, particularly in the light of the pressures they will have encountered as assistants and associates to meet ever-growing targets). As a measure that all can relate to, it has clear appeal. Its drawback is, however, that it reflects only one aspect of a partner's behaviour and activities and there is much more to being a partner than being a fee earner. Therefore, a system which rewards only billing will tend to antagonise those who do engage fully in the tasks of management, marketing, etc. Further, it does not allow for the fact that certain areas of work are likely to offer inherently more opportunities for fee earning on a large scale. For instance, if a partner recording 1,500 chargeable hours on family work were to bill less than a partner recording 1,100 hours on mergers and acquisitions work, would it be right to reward the latter for his output? Or should it be accepted that the firm's strategic decision was to encompass both types of work, so that input should be awarded just as much credit as output?

Distorting factors

There may be concerns that a particular measure might actually distort perceptions, or be counterproductive. Thus, if a partner's personal billing were the only, or chief, measure examined, this would potentially encourage:

- retention of work by that partner even when he could not cope with it, in terms of either expertise or capacity;
- failure to delegate work properly, or to supervise work once delegated; and
- lack of interest in any form of cross-selling.

A package of objective measures

What then of a package of measures? What if credit were given for both chargeable hours recorded and bills rendered? The next problem is to define what weight is attributed to each measure. So long as objective measures are adhered to, and a constant 'shopping basket' of those measures can be agreed, it is possible to agree a weighting pattern to be given to each. Further problems can arise however. The first is that questions might arise as to how valuable and reliable some such ostensibly objective measures are. Again, to use the above example, if the partner specialising in family law recorded chargeable hours of 1,500 but this consistently resulted in billing equivalent only to about 1,100 hours of other types of work, questions will be asked as to whether the difference is the result of the partner deliberately overstating the chargeable hours, or whether external restrictions such as fixed fee structures did not reward his genuine and properly-recorded efforts.

A broader package

The problem is that even a combination of objective measures cannot, by definition, take into account the many intangible efforts which partners may make for the firm's benefit. What, for instance, of the partner who spends every weekend on community-related efforts which may not only bring reflected glory to the firm, but may also lead to some direct client introductions. How is that effort to be recognised and encouraged? It is perfectly possible to devise a set of criteria which can be used to assess all sorts of behaviour, recognising different aspects of a firm's aspirations as to their partners' activities. One example of an attempt at this is shown in Figure 8.1.

Criteria	Factors to recognise
Personal financial performance	Billing; chargeable hours recorded; productivity (i.e. rate of conversion of chargeable hours to bills); fee collection
Client care	Efficient client service; client satisfaction; quality standards compliance; lack of complaints; client retention; developing personal expertise and recognition
Management	Overall firm management; financial management; office or departmental management; levels of responsibility; leadership; mentoring; training; delegation and supervision; non-chargeable hours recorded
Marketing	Development of existing worktypes; innovation; obtaining new clients; involvement in marketing initiatives; professional and community involvement

Figure 8.1   Criteria which may be used to assess performance of partners.

Judging broadly assessable performance

The big problem with this approach is that it inevitably introduces an element of subjectivity into the decision-making process. Someone has to take a view of performance across the board. This may be assisted by an efficiently run partner appraisal system, but nonetheless (unless the partnership is small enough for all partners to participate and flexible enough to accept a majority vote) someone is going to have the thoroughly unenviable task of sitting in judgement on their fellow partners, even if this results in a recommendation requiring full-partner endorsement rather than a binding decision.

Options for assessment methods

For those who face this task, there is no particular norm for how to approach it. In smaller firms it may simply be a task for the senior partner, perhaps after a consultation process. This may work if all concerned repose sufficient confidence in the ability of that individual to act impartially. Others may require a committee of some sort to consider the process. In larger firms, that committee may deliberately be divorced from the management committee or any equivalent, in order to avoid suspicions of partisanship. However, if this option is adopted, care needs to be taken that the committee is fully apprised of the firm's strategic objectives. In some cases, there may even be a right of appeal, if a particular partner feels aggrieved about the decision made in regard to his share.

Principles for successful performance related division

In short, performance-related profit sharing is a minefield. It may be a necessary minefield, but that does not make it any the less dangerous. No system will always suit everyone; nor will any decision on how much of the overall profit should be divided according to such principles. The key principles appear to be:

- Set a level for the proportion of profit to be divided according to performance measures which will allow genuine incentives, but not penalise others to an unacceptable level.
- Find a measure, or preferably a package of measures, which will reward strategically desirable behaviour.
- Consider how intangible inputs can be fairly reflected in the overall treatment.
- If an element of subjectivity of judgement is needed, find a universally acceptable method of assessing this.
- Above all, devise a system which is consistent.

'Eat what you kill'

General

The logical extreme of a performance-related system, where billing is the only output measure which is considered, is colloquially known as 'eat what you kill'. This philosophy is that only outputs matter, and that whatever must be done to obtain an output is a matter for that partner only. Thus whether an individual requires 1,000 or 1,500 hours of work to reach a certain billing level makes no difference. Clearly, this will develop, to an extreme extent, the potential disadvantages set out above. In effect, what would develop would be not so much a partnership, as a set of solicitors' chambers acting under the guise of a partnership. That is not to say that this is not a workable model for a business unit – clearly the Bar is the embodiment of such a process. What it does mean, however, is that there ceases to be any incentive for each member to act in the interest of his fellows (unless there is to be an element of distribution of work amongst the members, as is the case with the clerking system at the Bar). The logical consequence of that is that all activities such as management, marketing, etc., must be done centrally or outsourced unless they relate solely to the existing or particular clients of the individual member. Thus they will form part of the overheads of the business unit, and can accordingly be apportioned pro rata to income.

Drawbacks

One increasing difficulty of this sort of approach is related to capital investment which might be required by the unit. It is easy, for instance, to suggest that all members and staff of a chambers-type firm would need access to a basic word processor, the acquisition of which should be treated as a general expense to be shared as above. What, however, of specialist software to facilitate only, say, conveyancing work. Why should a litigation member pay a contribution towards that? If the operation is to proceed under the umbrella of a partnership, how can the participants (and, just as importantly, the accounts and tax computations relating to the partnership) cope with such inequality of investment? Thus, the 'eat what you kill' solution may not be as appealing in reality as it seems to be in theory.

Notes

1   Finance Act 1994 and subsequent Finance Acts introducing the self assessment scheme.
2   Bear in mind that an indemnity needs to be in writing to be valid.
3   One commentator argues that because a true partner, i.e. an equity partner, cannot be an employee of the partnership, and because s.4(4) of the Limited Liability Partnerships Act 2000 simply compares the LLP position to that of a partnership, it is not possible for a member of an LLP ever to be an employee: Blackett-Ord, M. (2002) *Partnership*, 2nd edn, Butterworths, paras 21–46. While acknowledging that the section is not very well worded, it is suggested that the intention is to allow salaried members in just the same way as salaried partners, i.e. people who are held out as having the full role but who in reality have not.
4   SI 2001/1090.
5   Mayson, S. *'Approaches to Profit-Sharing'*, Working Paper for Nottingham Law School.

9

Personal development

This chapter looks at those issues which are most central to the new partner as an individual. The idea of development as a reflective practitioner is explored, and the importance of focusing on personal goals is emphasised. The time management needs of a partner's multiple roles are expanded on, and these are taken into the requirement for project planning skills. Leadership skills are discussed, both in principle and in relation to tasks such as chairing meetings. The personal skills needed for a partner's tasks as coach, mentor, and leader of change are reviewed. Recognising a partner's marketing role, the skills needed for dealing with the public in terms of presentations, media handling, networking, etc. are examined. The problems of stress and stress management are investigated, and lastly the information management skills which the partner will need are reviewed.

Looking inward

The achievement of partnership

There is no doubt that, for the great majority of those who achieve promotion to partner, this will be a hugely significant step in their own personal development. The professional environment is generally highly competitive, and the struggle to obtain elevation will have taken several years, even if not all of that time has been spent within one firm. Many firms operate an 'up or out' policy, whether or not they are honest enough to articulate this, and so candidates for partnership will be aware that if they are unsuccessful they will be expected to move on to pastures new. The combative nature of the process of choosing new partners has led to its being referred to as the 'promotion to partner tournament'.[1] The problem with such single-minded concentration upon the attainment of partnership is that, in many cases, candidates will not have given thought to what lies beyond success, so that they will not have considered what their further personal goals are, or what personal skills they will need to develop in order to achieve those goals. The time of the change of status is therefore an appropriate time to reflect consciously and deliberately on this.

Work–life balance

Historically, one consequence of promotion has been that an already busy professional became an impossibly busy partner. On top of an expanding client caseload comes the burden of the management tasks and responsibilities which are discussed elsewhere in this book. Professionals who are, by nature, high achievers, and hence place great importance upon fulfilling what is expected of them, will do all they can to meet these increased demands. The consequence may be that personal and family life takes second place, and/or that stresses build up to a point where the new partner's health may be threatened. Increasingly, there is a recognition that personal needs and considerations should be given a greater prominence than has previously been the case. Charles Handy[2] quotes no less prosaic an organisation than the Department of Education as defining 'spirituality' as 'The valuing of the non-material aspects of life, and intimations of an enduring reality'. Some of the more enlightened firms recognise this in their partner selection processes, and will look for qualities such as the ability to 'switch off' from work.[3] Recognising a need, and altering engrained working patterns to cope with it, are two very different things, especially in an age when the tyranny of the mobile phone and the laptop computer mean that no professional can ever consider himself truly out of reach of the office unless he deliberately chooses to be.

Finding time to reflect

The process of consideration will require a conscious effort to find time to reflect on what is required for the future. This will not happen without planning. Unless a very determined effort is made to create this space, the day-to-day demands of professional life will mean that this task is put off for a later date. Each individual owes it to himself to invest time in his own future in this way and will have to find a way which is available to and suits him. Some individuals may be fortunate enough to have a mentor (in this particular case, preferably outside the firm in order to avoid any potential conflict) with whom they can discuss the position and their ideas. Others may prefer to set out their ideas on paper, even if only for a readership of one, and produce what is in effect a personal business plan, with issues not related to work included as part of the product/profit mix. Yet others may simply find there are certain environments where they are comfortable and which are conducive to reflection. The eminent judge and legal author Robert Megarry was fond of claiming that he had all his best ideas in the bath! The method chosen does not matter, but the act of undertaking the exercise does. Indeed, in a working paper entitled *The Future of the Professions*,[4] the Council for Excellence in Management and Leadership indicated, as one of seven main recommendations, that

'Managers and leaders . . . should explore techniques of reflection as a means of continually developing their roles so that professional work is supported and emerging dilemmas are managed in a complex and dynamic process'.

When should the chance to reflect be taken?

Ideally, the process of reflection should begin well before actual admission to partnership, and, at the latest, by the time that discussions about admission begin. This is simply so that issues which may become sticking points can be recognised and faced before too much commitment has been made. If the consequences of partnership will create problems which are so fundamental as to make the change in status undesirable, then it is much better that this is seen before the transition occurs. Equally, if there are questions which need to be explored in order to see whether personal plans can be accommodated within the partnership context, they should be looked at in order that any admission documentation can be framed appropriately. A classic illustration, in an era where there are currently more women than men being admitted as solicitors, is the question of what the attitude of existing (often all male) partners will be towards maternity leave and possibly flexible working hours. The question may simply never have been addressed before by the existing partners, but it should not be assumed that they will view the behaviour of their equity partners in the same way as they would that of members of staff.[5] Indeed new partners would do well to consider how their fellow partners may perceive the position of partners as differing from that of employees in respect of an ever-growing range of employee rights in respect of leave for paternal, parental, or family purposes, and rights to request flexible working hours and conditions. Partners can be very much harder on themselves than upon staff, and less forgiving of the wishes of a fellow partner in these areas.

Making reflection a continuous process

Once you have started considering your personal and professional situations and the relationship between them, you should endeavour to continue the process continuously. There is a cartoon of a bleary-eyed, slack-jowled, pyjama-clad man in his middle age peering unhappily at himself in the mirror in the morning and saying: 'To think, you're my sole means of support!' David Maister refined the idea somewhat when he referred[6] to looking at himself in the mirror, a year after commencing his career as a consultant, and asking himself what he had learned from that first year of operation. He and others recommend the keeping of a personal journal as a record of these exercises in self-analysis. There is no external reason why this document should not be combined with the record of training experiences which is required professionally, in the shape of a log of the hours of continuous professional development undertaken by each solicitor. This would be very much in keeping with one of the primary ideas underlying the Investors in People standard, which is that the individual and the organisation should evaluate all training received. Stephen Mayson, the chief architect of the Nottingham Law School MBA in Legal Practice, and his colleagues there (notably Ian McLachlan) have developed the concept of a 'reflective practitioner'. Mayson[7] uses the model set out below to show the circularity of the required process of questioning the outcome (in personal and emotional terms as well as technical success) of actions one has undertaken or been part of, considering what lessons are to be learned from them, working out how to apply them, and then testing their effect once put into practice.

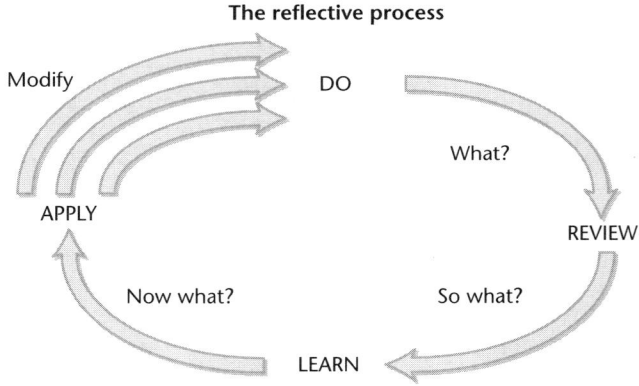

Figure 9.1   The reflective process.
Source: Mayson, S. (1997) *Making Sense of Law Firms* Blackstone Press. Reproduced by permission.

Aligning personal and strategic goals

Just as with other forms of business planning, successful personal planning in the partnership context requires alignment of each partner's personal goals with the strategic aims of the firm. If there is a fundamental mismatch, the result will only be harmful to each party. Thus if, for instance, a candidate for partnership in a global law firm wants to spend more time with his family, but the reality of the offer on the table is that he will be involved in international transactions requiring him to spend extensive periods away from home, then a mutually satisfactory result can hardly be expected. That may be an extreme example, but there will be many other ways in which it will be important to examine the extent to which a partner will be able to reconcile the attainment of personal objectives with the pursuit of the firm's long-term business aims. Thus a partner to whom the intellectual challenge of ever more complex work is an essential motivator is unlikely to be content within a firm which, say, wishes him to take on the role of a manager of bulk 'commodity' work.

Aligning values

The first aim is to ensure a match between what the individual and the firm want to achieve. However, whether or not there is similar accord as to how that should be done is quite another problem. The 'culture' of a firm is difficult to define, and as hard to change as the path of the proverbial supertanker. If there is a substantive difference between the values of the existing partners, as demonstrated by the firm's culture, and the values of the incoming partner, there will be problems ahead. Reference is made at pp. 163–164 to the relationship between cultural issues and success factors. The incoming partner would do well to consider how many of the indices apparently concomitant with success are genuinely and demonstrably held by the firm's partners, and how they match up with his own views. For instance, a prospective partner who believes wholeheartedly in the idea that the firm's activities should be client-driven will face problems when entering a partnership where the partners, who may publicly espouse this theory, still hold the old-fashioned view that clients are really a nuisance who interfere with the real work that needs to be done.

Obtaining the data to reflect upon

No process of examination will be adequate or rewarding without the right data. This will consist of the subjective responses of the individual to circumstances he has encountered, but will present only part of the picture. To take it further, there will need to be a conscious process of obtaining the views of others, who may include mentors, partners, staff senior and junior, clients, and other involved third parties such as fellow professional advisers on a client's team. The process of obtaining their views can be quite natural and mutually beneficial, and if conducted casually is more likely to arouse interest than hostility. It will nonetheless take a deliberate personal effort to conduct a 'wash-up' exercise at the end of each major transaction, to test not only the objective outcomes, but also the subjective perceptions of the experience for those participating, and how they could be improved in future.

Focusing the market-related questions

Some consistency in the approach to this process, year-on-year, is probably desirable, not least to enable the assessment of how well aims have been achieved. In his work, as noted above, Maister concludes his chapter on the subject with the list of questions in Figure 9.2 below.

In what way are you personally more valuable on the marketplace than last year?

What are your plans to make yourself more valuable on the marketplace than last year?

What specific new skills do you plan to acquire or enhance in the next year?

What's your personal strategic plan for your career over, say, the next three years?

What can you do to make yourself (even more) special on the market in the near future?

What, precisely, is it that you want to be famous for?

Figure 9.2   Market-related questions.

Source: Maister, D. (1993) *Managing the Professional Service Firm*, Free Press, New York. Reproduced by permission.

Focusing the personal questions

The authors whose work underpins the well known Harvard Business School course for managers of professional service firms, Jay W. Lorsch and Thomas J. Tierney, stress the importance for each individual of taking charge of his personal destiny by asking questions about his personal situation, and taking decisions accordingly.[8] Their colleagues Robert S. Kaplan and David P. Norton in the mid-1990s devised the concept of the 'Balanced Scorecard',[9] as a means of tying in an agreed package of key performance measurements to a firm's strategy. They have recently assessed how that concept has been developed in real life by businesses which have adopted it. Kaplan and Norton have stressed the proven need for measures which are to be adopted for the formulation of an individual's personal 'Balanced Scorecard' to be aligned with the strategic goals of the firm [10] It might be as well to add some further questions, along the lines of:

- How do the answers to the above questions tie in with what the firm expects of me?
- How do they fit in with the firm's strategic goals and values?
- What position do I want my role as partner to hold in relation to my life outside the office?
- How do the above answers fit in with the need to balance my personal future?

Evaluating your personal training needs

One of the questions posed above refers to the acquisition or enhance-
ment of skills. This should be regarded as applying as much to personal
skills as to technical ones, i.e. to the concept of the skills required in order
to undertake the relevant tasks, rather than the technical aspects of the
tasks themselves. The next stage, therefore, is to consider what those skills
may be. In effect, this involves asking what particular abilities a partner
will need which either will have to be deployed at an intensity not previously required in the capacity of an associate, or are completely new. The
list will of course differ for every individual, but amongst those likely to
feature will be:

- *Time management* – to cope with the new variety of roles and their
  demands.
- *Presentational skills* – for occasions such as seminars, tender
  opportunities, and in-house meetings.
- *Chairing meetings* – to move forward departmental and team meetings.
- *Marketing techniques** – developing the entrepreneurial aspects of a
  partner's role.
- *Networking* – spreading the firm's message in a variety of informal
  settings.
- *Leadership* – inspiring the team and carrying it along with you.
- *Delegation and supervision* – controlling and fostering the growth of
  the team.
- *Mentoring and coaching* – using your talents to develop others
  individually.
- *Managing stress*.
- *Human resources management** – maximising the potential of the most
  important resource available.
- *Financial and accounting knowledge** – making sense of the information
  presented.
- *IT skills* – if new areas of IT talents are needed to cope with items not
  met before, e.g. accounting spreadsheets.

Some of these areas (marked above with an asterisk) are dealt with elsewhere in this book as separate chapters. The others are looked at here,
being essentially the personal skills that partners will need to develop for
themselves.

Time management

The principles of time management

There are effectively two aspects of time management, though often only one is recognised. The first is the way in which time is allocated between tasks, i.e. an exercise in prioritising various actions, and apportioning time in the working day accordingly. The second, which is less often carried out and which requires more depth of thought, is to analyse exactly what is inherently required for tasks to be carried out and to ask not where that fits into the working schedule, but rather how the time required can be reduced so as to create more space in the schedule.

Knowing what needs to be managed

Like most aspects of management, a fundamental of effective planning in the field of time management is to know what the time requirements actually are. This should not be, and need not be, a matter of guesswork. Most firms now have computerised time recording systems, but these are often underused when it comes to non-chargeable time, which the new partner needs to take especially into account. Many will regard the recording of such time as an irritation at best, or a waste of time at worst. The categories used for analysis may or may not mean anything. In reality, however, this system, if properly used, can be the key to a partner's understanding of how his time is actually being spent, which can then be used as the basis for planning.

The first thing a partner should do is to start recording *all* time in a manner which will yield meaningful data, so that he knows, for instance, how much time regularly has to be spent in supervising and monitoring his team; or in reading papers distributed prior to regular partners' meetings; or in preparing and presenting seminars. Guesswork is simply not sufficient, and will mean that every time a managerial task comes up either the time required will be underestimated, and result in a last minute panic, or it will be overestimated, and so just put off. Every partner owes it to himself and to others to use the tools available to build up as accurate a picture as possible of what is actually required of him.

Time management for partners

The chances are that, by the stage he becomes a partner, a lawyer will already have had some training in the basic time management skills required as a fee earner, e.g. dividing the day into dedicated sections to allow time to delegate work properly to a secretary and any subordinates, time to speak to clients, time to concentrate undisturbed on drafting, etc. If no such training has been received, then an excellent exposition of the techniques required is to be found in Chapter 6 of Matthew Moore's book *Quality Management for Law Firms*.[11] Part of the problem, however, is that all such techniques have their limitations,[12] such as their inherent conflict with the much-avowed principles of accessibility for clients and an open door for colleagues. These issues have been greatly exacerbated by the advent of direct-dial telephones, removing the defensive 'shield' of the receptionist, and by e-mail which anticipates an instant response. The added difficulty for partners is that there is a very significant element of time required to allow for managerial responsibilities. Further, while some of those requirements will be for active time (i.e. time when the partner is to undertake a specific task) much will be of a passive nature (i.e. when others will, without warning, decide that they need some of the partner's time in order to be able to perform their own tasks). In many ways, the latter is more difficult to plan for than the former.

Managing partners' expectations

George Orwell, in *1984*, coined the term 'doublethink' for the ability to hold two diametrically opposite views simultaneously. He might have been writing of the expectations of existing partners as to how a new partner will deal with his client base. On the one hand, they will expect him to take on a range of new tasks which will necessarily entail reducing the time spent on client work or increasing the overall amount of time devoted to the firm. On the other they will expect him to expand his and his team's billing. That is a circle which some partners never manage to square. The only way in which it is possible to accomplish the two aims together is to work differently, rather than more. The partner will have to learn to delegate more of his work (subject to control of delegation – see pp. 47–48) and, in order to do so, will have to consider carefully which aspects of his work do not require direct personal involvement, while he remains the main point of contact with the client. In fact, in doing so, a partner is also fulfilling one of the underlying financial requirements of a firm, as indicated by Mayson,[13] namely that an equity partner, to justify his existence, needs to generate sufficient work to sustain not only himself but also a sufficient number of assistant staff, in order to maintain the leverage principles which underlie the growth of profit per equity partner.

Coping with colleagues' demands

One aspect of taking on a partner's role is that colleagues will expect more of you. Those who are your new partners will want time to find your opinion on matters that they would not previously have discussed with you. More work will be delegated by you to fee earners around you, with naturally greater time requirements for you to review matters with them.

Staff generally will assume (rightly or wrongly) that you will have extra administrative and managerial decision-taking powers, and will wish to consult you or simply sound off on all the topics under the sun. How then to cope with such demands? Some matters need to be recognised, and some ground rules need to be established and understood by all. Some basic examples are:

- Recognise that those occasions when clear, uninterrupted, time is needed will be at both more difficult than ever to arrange, and also more essential, since periods of clear thinking time will be needed for you to develop your approach to your managerial responsibilities.
- Work out what arrangements will suit you best for such quiet times. If the reality is that such times will not be possible within the office and normal working hours, then recognise this and plan them accordingly, e.g. by working at home or by scheduling planned periods in the office before or after the normal working day, when interruptions will be minimal.
- Structure, so far as possible, those occasions when others will want your time. For instance, have a regular morning team meeting, when everyone knows they can discuss any problems which have arisen, avoiding a constant stream of people popping their heads around the door.
- For all those who need your input on a substantial basis, whether it be a secretary who needs instructions, or a fee earner to whom you have delegated work and who needs support and supervision, set aside times when they know that they can freely access you.
- Having established those principles, do not try to operate a constant 'open-door' policy. There is a world of difference between being genuinely approachable but on a planned basis, and claiming to have an open door but being in fact so chaotically disorganised that you radiate resentment whenever anyone asks to speak to you.
- Acknowledge the fact that no system will ever be perfect. There will always be the partner who pops in, or the fee earner who needs emergency help, or the court list that means you are not around when planned. When such events happen, be careful to respect the pressures that your unpredictability may place upon others who are trying to manage their own routines. Do not fall into the trap of promising to be available at certain times and consistently failing to honour those promises, thus building a reputation for having insufficient respect for the work and time of others. Afford internal appointments exactly the same respect that you would for client meetings. If there is a genuine reason for delay or even cancellation, inform the other party as soon as possible of the reason for the problem, be proactive in making substitute arrangements, and be absolutely certain to comply with them.

Project management

An aspect of management which may be considered as a specialist sub-set of time management is project management. Partners will inevitably, whether they realise it or not, have had some involvement in project management, since that is, in effect, what the management of a client's case requires, i.e. knowing the stages through which a matter needs to progress, evaluating the resources which will be needed to carry it out, and establishing a timescale for the conduct of the matter which satisfies both external imperatives and internal wishes. They may well not, however, have had any formal training in such techniques. Now, as partners, they may be involved in the formulation and supervision of non-client projects which require the application of proper management techniques. Aspects in respect of which partners may become involved include:

- Identifying when project management techniques become needed, i.e. where there is a defined set of linked actions needed to accomplish a goal over a period of time.
- Putting together the team to carry out the task.
- Determining the precise nature of the steps required.
- Allocating to each step:
    - a period of time for its completion;
    - the resources (money, technology, people, know-how) needed; and
    - a responsible supervisor.
- Setting out the sequence of events (which may of course overlap in part).
- Allowing for contingencies.
- Providing a monitoring mechanism for the progress of the project against constraints of time, budget, quality, etc. (and in turn allocating resources to this checking procedure).

A common project management technique is the use of a Gantt chart. An example is shown in Figure 9.3 overleaf. This shows graphically the timing and interdependency of the various steps involved. If more sophistication is needed, there are various software tools available.

Accountability and failure

One of the psychological barriers that any new partner must cross is coming to accept the extent to which he is accountable. Previously, he will of course have had to get used to certain levels of accountability, whether this was to clients, their supervising partners, or to external agencies such as the courts. Generally speaking, however, such accountability will have

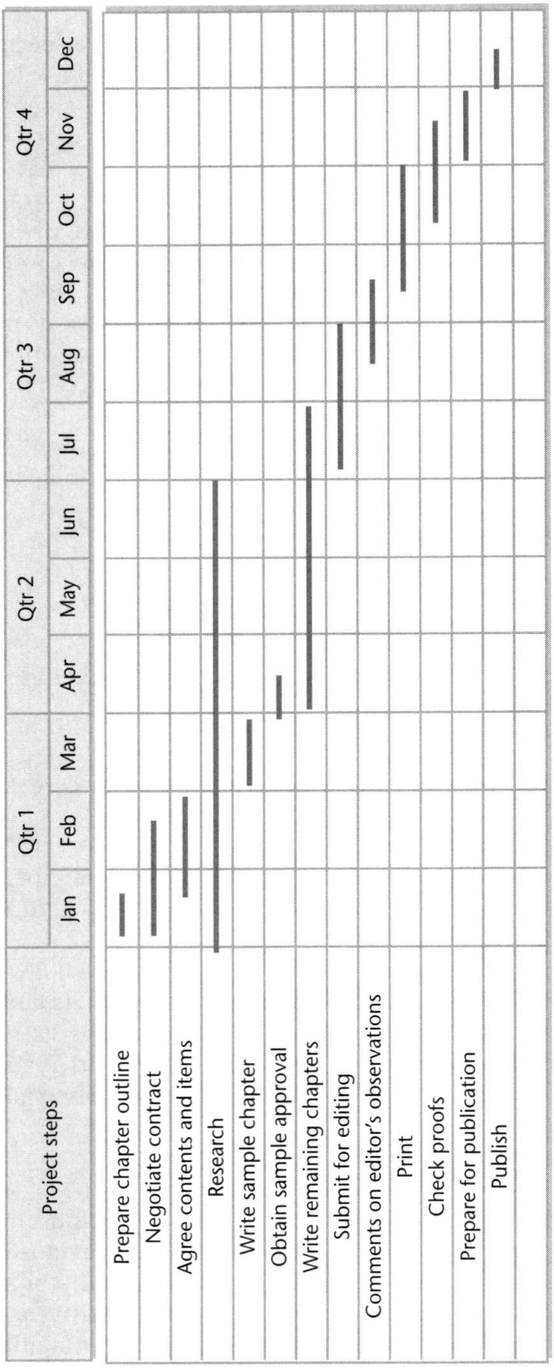

Figure 9.3 Example of a Gantt chart, based on a fictional book proposal.

been focused on client work. Now, as a partner, he must accept the concept that he is responsible for a great many more things, and to a great many more people. Any decisions taken with regard to time management, and the prioritisation of tasks that entails, must therefore be taken with that in mind, and the partner needs to recognise that he will be held accountable for any failures. Thus, repeated protestations that he has been too busy to carry out management tasks delegated to him will affect perceptions of his success as a partner (and hence, possibly, his future career path). Failure to provide sufficient time for staff will lead them to a position where he is accorded little or no respect as a manager, and thus will receive no support when it counts. Failure to nurture his client relationships will mean that the strategic goal of his promotion has failed. Once that hurdle of perception has been crossed, time management will be given the thought and importance it deserves.

Learning to work with people

The necessary skills

Many of the tasks traditionally associated with the management and development of people are dealt with in Chapter 6 of this book. What falls to be considered here, however, are the personal skills that a partner needs to develop within himself in order to fulfil all aspects of his managerial responsibilities. These include: a look at the principles of leadership; some pointers on chairing meetings; an overview of the tasks of delegation and supervision; and the development of skills of mentoring and coaching.

The importance of leadership

The subject of leadership is one on which there have been countless books written,[14] and of which there is continual study.[15] The one thing upon which there can be no doubt is the importance of leadership in producing real bottom-line results. David Maister, in the research for his book *Practice What You Preach*,[16] set out to analyse which of 74 factors affecting the culture of firms correlated with the financial success of those firms. To his surprise, he found that there were nine factors which on statistical analysis appeared to be not merely correlative, but actually causative of success. In other words, they were factors which of themselves were likely to lead firms to success. Four of them directly concerned leadership, i.e.:

- 'Management gets the best work out of everybody in the office.'

- 'We invest a significant amount of time in things that will pay off in the future.'
- 'People within our office always treat others with respect.'
- 'The quality of supervision on client projects is uniformly high.'

In his experience as a member of a regional panel for the validation of applications for the award of the status of Investor In People, the author has observed that the one constant theme which emerges from assessors' reports on successful organisations (whether these be large or small, public sector or private) is that the quality of individual leadership within these organisations is high.

Becoming a leader

It may be true in some cases that great leaders are born, not made. It would however be entirely wrong to assume that some of the attitudes and patterns of behaviour common to good leaders cannot be taught, self-taught, or simply absorbed. What then may some of those features be? An exhaustive list is not possible, but some of the main characteristics are set out below.

- *Continually developing professional competence*. It is almost a given that, to become a partner, a high degree of technical professional competence should have to be shown. Simply maintaining that level will not, however, be enough. The successful leading partner will demonstrate through his actions that he is constantly striving to expand and develop his professional knowledge. This is done not just by undertaking progressively more complex cases, but also by keeping ahead of the changes in the law and showing awareness of such changes for the dynamics of the firm's operations, and being concious of the business opportunities that changes may offer. Being visibly willing to share and disseminate that developing knowledge to all for the benefit of the firm and the individuals within it is also a key factor. Another of David Maister's[17] nine causative indicators of success is: 'We have no room for those who put their personal agenda ahead of the interests of the client or the office.'
- *Having and communicating a clear strategic vision for the business*. Put simply, people like to know where they are going. To that end, they need to know that the leader has a clear idea of what the future of the business, or the relevant unit within it, will be, and second they need to be told what that goal is. They cannot be expected to work towards a goal of which they are ignorant. One of the IIP indicators is: 'The organisation has a plan with clear aims and objectives, which are understood by everyone.' Staff need to know what parts they are

expected to play in the future of the firm, and how their contributions are to be assessed and measured.

One characteristic often attributed to a successful leader is that he is 'inspirational'. This is impossible to define, but it would seem reasonable to assume that staff are unlikely to be inspired by anyone who does not have a demonstrable enthusiasm for, and powerful commitment to, the growth and success of the business. That cannot really be shown unless staff understand the aims at which that dedication is directed.

- *Knowing how to get the best out of people.* Elsewhere in this book (see Chapter 6) reference is made to the assessment of colleagues' talents and attitudes when it comes to team building. This is simply a specific illustration of the general principle that a good leader has to play to his strengths, and to appreciate the abilities of those around him. He needs to motivate them to push the boundaries of those abilities, but not at the cost of imposing unacceptable workloads or strains which will cause stress or similar problems. He will know what form of incentive will work best for particular individuals, and will recognise the importance of frequent encouragement by talking up genuine contributions. He will also appreciate the vital nature of an early assessment of the real reasons underlying any shortcomings in performance, rather than simply criticising failure without investigation of what it reveals.

- *Knowing and communicating with the staff.* It will be impossible for any leader to get the best out of someone who is unknown to them, especially when surrounded by often highly individualistic professionals who are unlikely to respond well to unreasoned commands from on high. The successful leader needs to know his team well, and to be a frequent and known presence to them in turn, hence the coining of the phrase 'Management By Walking About' (and its acronym 'MBWA'). It seems straightforward to say that a leader should know those he is leading, but in many cases, especially with offices which have segmented areas (or, worse still, are physically apart) this will require a very deliberate effort to achieve. It is made easier if some way of building this into a routine can be devised. Other means of communication of course should also be deployed, and these should be mixed (rather than becoming dependent on one method) and should be as personal as possible. Beware the de-personalising effect of a culture of communication by memo or general e-mail.

- *Being a good listener.* Lawyers are often not instinctively good listeners. They are brought up to record instructions carefully, which can mean that all the speaker sees of them is the top of their heads as they scribble away. They are also well aware that time is money, and hence are inclined to try to bring the speaker back to what they perceive as being the heart of the problem. They want to advise rather than hear.

All of these are inimical to being a good listener in managerial terms, since it is often the fact of listening which is as important as what is being said. If notes are to be taken, this should only be done after the speaker has already been through his story. Pauses should be an occasion for prompting with an open question, not for interjecting with a view. This is not to say that the listener should not offer a view, or indicate a willingness to act on what is being said, but rather that the speaker needs to be given full opportunity to express his concerns first. Remember that the fact that a perception may, on the facts, be unjustified, does not lessen the strength of that perception or the importance of dealing with it properly.

The listener should be careful not to react too instinctively. If time for consideration will be required, the reasons for this should be made clear, and an indication of a timescale within which a substantive response can be given should be provided and adhered to. If action can be agreed upon, ensure that it is clear who is to do what, and when any action is to be done. If a request has to be declined, or a view disagreed with, a clear and reasoned argument should be given. Try to ensure consistency of response, not only from oneself but across the firm, especially when dealing with sensitive issues such as working practices and rights, where the ability of a rash answer to cause dissent is enormous. Try to end every such interview by taking the colleague along with your viewpoint. As President Eisenhower put it: 'Pull the string, and it will follow wherever you wish. Push it, and it will go nowhere at all.'

- *Gaining the trust of staff.* One essential for any leader is that staff trust him. A study[18] in 1997 indicated that this ranked highest in a list of leadership attributes. A leader will not be able to motivate those around him, and be able to take them in the direction he wishes, unless they are prepared to accept that he can be depended on to make choices which are correct and fair. Trust is not something that can be learned, but it can be earned. A partner will go a long way towards gaining that trust if he:

  - is consistent and fair in decision-making;
  - continually involves himself in the development of others;
  - ensures that staff are involved with clients;
  - entrusts staff with tasks which will stretch them;
  - works with staff when difficulties are encountered;
  - gives clear recognition of a job well done;
  - keeps people informed about what is happening throughout the business;
  - champions his team in all reasonable ways; and
  - lives up to the set of values that he ostensibly espouses.

Chairing meetings

Leadership skills come to the fore when chairing any meeting. Once again, this comes more naturally to some than to others (see Chapter 6) but can nonetheless become an acquired skill, by using the techniques below.

- Ensure that the meeting has been properly prepared for. That means not only that the chair has prepared himself, but that he has checked and cajoled beforehand to ensure that all others are up to scratch.
- Encourage punctuality, and reward it on the part of those who do turn up on time by starting promptly, and not wasting their time by indulging those whose disrespect for their colleagues is shown by the fact that they arrive late.
- Have a clear agenda, and obtain the initial agreement of the meeting to the scope of the subjects that are to be covered, and the points upon which decisions are to be taken.
- Set a time limit for the meeting generally, and allocate (even if not publicly) blocks of time to each agenda item.
- Do not assume – unless you know it to be the case – that all present at the meeting know each other. In the case of inter-disciplinary meetings in particular, introductions by the chair may be needed. Consider whether name cards in front of places, or name badges, may be appropriate.
- Make sure that all present have the chance to contribute, while keeping the discussion on a pertinent track, and not overindulging those who feel obliged to comment on every point under discussion, whether they have anything useful to contribute or not.
- Maintain decorum throughout. It is not unknown for tempers to become frayed in meetings, and for aggressive or even bullying stances to be adopted. It is the chair's job to avoid such a situation, and to make clear to all that unacceptable behaviour will not be tolerated.
- Plant ideas. If the chair knows the direction in which he wants the discussion to go, it is often better for him to make an observation which leads others to suggest his preferred course of action than for him to make the suggestion himself. This will boost the confidence of the person who does come up with the successful idea, and will make all members of the group feel that it is their collective participation which is driving the group's achievements, rather than adoption of the chair's personal agenda.
- Make sure that when every decision is taken, a record is kept of that decision, who will be responsible for its implementation, and within what timescale it is to be completed.
- Ensure that, after the meeting, a record of those points is distributed promptly, by way of an action list, even if more formal minutes are

to follow later. That record can often form the basis of the group's next agenda, thus both ensuring consistency and simplifying the task next time around.

- Try to arrange matters so that the tasks which fall out of the meeting's decisions are evenly spread among the members, and that the jobs given to each group member are suitable for them, taking into account their characteristics and talents for group performance (see Chapter 6).

- Try to ensure a comfortable physical environment for the meeting. Cramped, airless rooms with uncomfortable seating and no refreshments will not produce the same results as a meeting held in a well-lit and comfortable area, where everyone has space to lay out their papers, and refreshments are available. Looking after team members' comfort will help them to feel that their function, as a group, is important to the organisation. Also avoid the situation where too many people are spread out down one long table, so that it is impossible for those at one end to hear speakers at the other. Stay away from rooms where there are frequent external noises, or which can only be kept at a reasonable temperature by excessively noisy air conditioning.

- Ensure the meeting is as free from interruption as possible. The more difficult the meeting, the more important this becomes. In the office you are always vulnerable to the person who pops their head round the door. In some cases, you may wish to take the meeting out of the office environment altogether, and use an external venue to avoid interruptions. Announce at the outset that mobile phones and pagers should be switched off for the duration of the meeting.

- If someone has any particular role to play, e.g. by making a presentation at the meeting, check that he is fully rehearsed and prepared, and that any handouts or audio-visual aids are present and working.

- If outsiders are to attend a particular part of the meeting only, make sure that suitable arrangements are made for their reception and introduction.

- Try to finish the meeting on an upbeat note, so that all concerned leave feeling they have achieved something, that they know why and when the group is next to meet, and that they look forward to that meeting.

Delegation and supervision

Techniques for delegation and supervision are set out at some length in Chapter 3. Some training, and almost certainly some changes in attitude, will be necessary if the new partner is to delegate and supervise to the best advantage of himself and all those around him. The feeling that time spent in supervising is not 'real work' is hard for many to shift, but it is absolutely essential in the modern office environment that this time is given willingly, with full recognition of the benefits it brings.

Coaching

Delegation and supervision bring the partner and those fee earners working with him into frequent contact, and is the ideal relationship for coaching, even if this is never articulated between the parties. The new partner should be willing to use his talents to bring on others – indeed he should be keen to do so, not only out of pride in his own achievements, but because he will thus make a major contribution to the growth of what Mayson refers to as the 'know-how capital' of the firm.[19] Coaching is one of those rare opportunities in life where one can claim both selfish and philanthropic motives. With respect to the first, the partner is building up the ability of his assistants to cope (and to help him) with more complex work and to contribute to the firm's overall reputation and expertise. For the second, he is putting something back into the profession which has brought him (almost inevitably after similar help from someone senior to him) to his current position. Coaching does not have to be formal, but it may benefit from discussion of the skills the assistant needs to acquire. The partner can then delegate work to ensure that the person being coached acquires hands-on experience in those areas, with the necessary assistance, in the requisite areas.

Mentoring

Mentoring has some matters in common with coaching, but also certain differences. Mentoring is best developed as a long-term relationship, which may last for many years. Since it is more to do with the personal development of an individual than with technical skills, it is less likely to depend upon a line-management connection than coaching. For instance, some firms will construct mentoring programmes which deliberately link partners in one discipline with assistants from another. The perceived advantages are that the assistant may feel more free to express personal views and concerns than he would to a line manager, and that he will benefit from a perspective of the firm and the profession which is different from that within his department or professional discipline, thus broadening his experience. Like coaching, there may be little formality about the creation of mentoring arrangements, or equally the firm may have a policy of making deliberate arrangements.

A mentor's responsibilities are to ensure the general welfare and development of his charge, identifying needs in terms of personal skills, exposure to types of work, non-technical training requirements, and ensuring that the career path of his mentee through the firm is as smooth as possible. Once again, there are mixed motives for undertaking this task. An assistant who feels he counts as a person within the firm will be far more likely to stay with it. The mentor should welcome the opportunity to pass on the compliment that a senior partner has probably paid to him in the past by taking the time and trouble to be interested in his development. Personal chemistry will be of especial importance (hence the difficulty of formalising the process) and the relationship will be heavily dependent on trust.

Recognising those whom a decision will affect

One of the least instinctive aspects of making decisions that affect others is to work methodically through the range of people who may be affected by what you do. To illustrate, consider a request from one secretary in a department to be allowed to leave work an hour early every day to pick up a child from school. It may seem that the decision will simply affect you and her, but in fact the following people will all have a view on your decision:

- All other secretaries in the department. They may have had previous similar requests turned down, or they may be watching to see what implications there are for them.
- The secretary's family. You may feel they should be beyond your need to consider, but if they are dissatisfied, pressures from them could affect the secretary's future attitudes and loyalty.
- The fee earner for whom the secretary works. Most offices have the ritual of signing off work in order to catch the evening post. How will it affect the fee earner's own routine if he has to bring that forward an hour?
- Support staff elsewhere in the firm. They may be watching to make sure one department does not get privileges denied to them.
- Your partners. They may be concerned at the knock-on effects of your decision, and will be keen to know what the financial consequences may be, i.e. whether there will be a reduction in the secretary's pay to compensate.

It is important to make a properly informed decision by considering all these groups of people before giving your response. If necessary, illustrate the people concerned in a diagram, as below in Figure 9.4.

Managing people through the process of change

The need to be able to demonstrate all the qualities discussed above will be at its greatest during a period of major change. Change management is a subject with a literature all of its own, and there are many theories as to how to cope best with change. The two points which appear to be

Figure 9.4   The typical groups of people who may be affected by your decision.

universally accepted are that people do not like change, as the uncertainties which it brings are frightening to them; and that the pace of change within the legal profession is likely to increase rather than diminish, so that the need for successful change management will also increase.

Views on the most efficient method for this process differ greatly. Some will advocate, at one end of a continuum, that so-called 'top-down' management is needed, to give a clear direction. Others suggest the contrary. A study for the Council for Excellence in Management and Leadership[20] suggests that:

> Command and control models of management and leadership have only a limited and partial place in professional organisations and the management of professional work. Over-emphasis on command and control is likely to engender low trust and alienation among professionals leading to lower levels of commitment and confidence.

At the other end of the continuum is the idea that staff should be as involved as possible in the formulation of the policy and the details of the change, to get them to 'buy-in' to the concept. Opponents would argue that the time taken by this process, and the consequent compromises entered into in order to obtain consensus, will fatally wound the chances of a programme of successful, radical, reform. Again, how far should change go? Some would argue for incremental change, but others would contend that only change which is total has any chance of success. Proponents of the latter theory have coined the term 'Business

Process Re-Engineering'.[21] There is no simple solution, and a partner charged with conducting any programme of change management will have to select the technique he thinks most appropriate. For a new partner, that decision may of course be taken at a higher level. It may assist the choice to know the stages which people pass through when involved with the process of change, illustrated in the model[22] below, used by Cranfield School of Management as the core of their general management programmes.

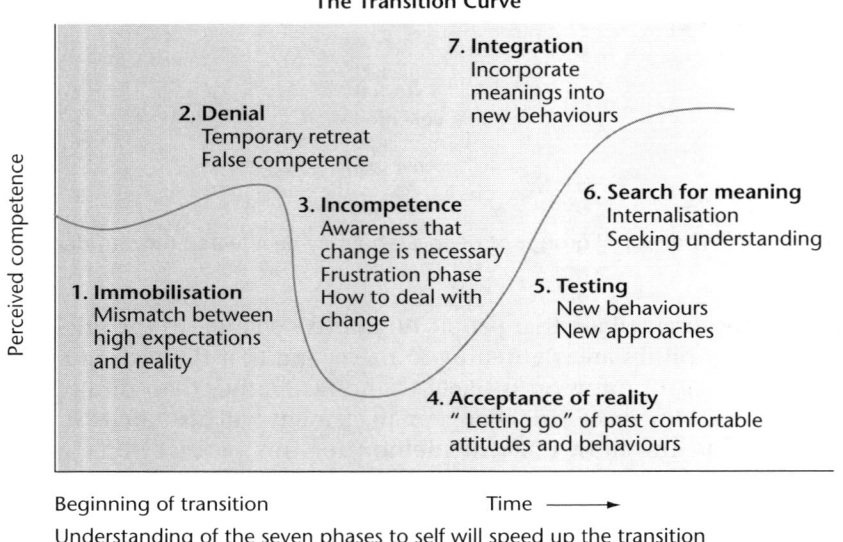

Figure 9.5   The seven stages in the transition cycle.
Source: Lambert, R. 'A Cycle of Change' (1993) Working Paper for Cranfield School of Management. Reproduced by permission.

Personal skills for marketing

General

Marketing techniques are examined elsewhere in this book (see Chapter 5). What falls to be considered here are the personal abilities which will be needed in order to make good use of those techniques. The likelihood is that, before attaining partnership, most lawyers will have had some exposure to marketing efforts, in the sense of putting themselves before the public, whether in general terms or with regard to specific actual or potential clients. After becoming a partner, however, the expectations of them will increase markedly, and they need to be ready to take on much more of a front role. This section will look at three aspects in particular, namely presentational skills, dealing with the media, and networking.

Making presentations

The need for a partner to make a presentation to a group of people may arise in a number of ways. He may give a seminar on a technical aspect of his work, perhaps to a group of current and prospective clients, or to a professional association such as a local law society. He may be asked to speak about the profession generally, for instance to a community group such as a Lions Club, Rotary Club or Round Table. He may make a direct pitch for work after being shortlisted from a tender process by a likely client. In all these scenarios, the same problems will arise, and the same basic steps will need to be taken. Much of the difficulty has to do with simple confidence. Even when a speaker knows his subject backwards, it can be difficult to persuade him that people will actually want to hear him, and that he will be able to put the subject over in a convincing way. The problem will be compounded by the fact that, at some time or other, all prospective speakers will have suffered the torture of sitting in the audience for speakers who are manifestly incompetent!

Presentation techniques

A number of simple practical points are set out below, although it will not always be possible to follow them all. For instance, if you are given a couple of days to prepare a tender, and arrive not knowing who your audience is going to be, where you are going to be speaking, or how long you are being asked to present for, then obviously there has to be a lot which is decided upon the fly. If however you are giving a seminar which your firm is organising, conditions will be much more conducive to a planned approach. It is advisable for a new partner to get a few occasions of the latter sort under his belt before he is likely to be exposed to the former, in order to gain the confidence that undoubtedly comes from practice.

Some ways in which confidence can be built are:

- Make preparations in the general sense of critiquing speakers to whom you are exposed – what techniques do they deploy and are these successful? Make a note (perhaps in your reflective journal as suggested above) so you can cherry-pick the best presentation ideas when it comes to your turn.
- Give yourself as much time as possible for the preparation of the event. Nothing is more likely to fluster the inexperienced speaker than knowing that he did not write his notes until the last moment.
- Avoid at all costs the temptation to commit the classic error of simply reading, word for word, a speech you have written out.

- Prepare notes in a form that will suit you. Some like to write out more or less the entire speech, as the mere act of writing forces them to focus their arguments. If doing this, however, the previous point needs to be kept very firmly in mind. Some prefer just summaries, and others merely headings. Whatever suits, try to find and highlight a trigger comment which, if you do happen to lose your way, will act as a rapid reminder of what comes next.
- Bear in mind that your notes are for you, not for the audience. They may therefore differ in depth from (though they should follow the running order of) either any fuller notes you have written (e.g. where conference organisers ask for a paper to distribute) or any slides you have prepared, using overhead projection or Microsoft PowerPoint ®. Some speakers may, however, deliberately choose to use such slides as their notes.
- Check with the organiser the time for which you are expected to speak.
- Test the length of your own presentation, and adjust if necessary to fit the organiser's requirements. There is no way of doing this other than by reading it aloud. Think about the pace at which you want to speak.
- Try the presentation out on some of your colleagues, and ask them for feedback on any good or bad points. Do this in time to allow any adjustments to be made, again without feeling rushed.
- Get to the venue early. This is essential so that you can, in your own good time, check a number of practical points, such as:
    - The type of microphone you will use. If this is not a fixed one, then your ability to manipulate notes will be hampered. If it is particularly directional, you may need to guard against moving your head too much. Check how far away you should stand for optimum effect.
    - Whether you will be using a lectern. If so, will it have room for a laptop (which you may well find placed there even if you are not using one yourself), your notes and any other items you may want to refer to? Is there a glass of water for you, in case you literally dry up at any time?
    - Whether any handouts you have prepared have been correctly distributed.
    - Whether any software is actually working on the computer it is supposed to! The number of speakers who have been frustrated by failure in this regard is legion. If possible, take your own laptop, and a copy of any program/file you are using on disk as well.
    - Who will be introducing you?
    - Where you will be placed before you rise to speak?

– If you will not be the first to speak, how are other speakers being received, and how are they coping with the environment as to acoustics, PA system, slide show, etc.?

- Avoid wandering or fidgeting.
- Try to enjoy the occasion! This may sound odd, but there is no doubt that a speaker's level of relaxation is conveyed to an audience. It is, after all, a chance to show off all the knowledge you have worked so hard to accumulate.
- If you know that questions are to be called for, consider planting one or two by talking beforehand to sympathetic members of the audience, to get the discussion going (or ask the chairman if he has already done so).
- Find out afterwards how the audience felt the presentation went. Many organised events will have audience feedback forms. If so, make sure that the organisers pass the results to you. It is useful to know not only what they thought of you, but what they thought of the event generally and the other speakers, so you can compare that with your own opinions of the venue, etc. and the techniques of the other speakers, and you can feed that information into the reflective loop referred to above.

Dealing with the media

The incoming partner should be aware of the firm's policy in dealing with the media. It may be that, for risk management reasons, the firm has a policy that only selected (and, possibly, trained) personnel are authorised to make any media comment. If however there is no such policy, or if events in practice override it, then the likelihood is that at some stage of their careers many partners will be called upon to contribute in some way to a media effort to produce an article, an interview, a programme, etc. Indeed, it is a very positive step to develop good relations with the media, especially on a localised or specialised basis, if this will be a straight-forward way of getting good publicity for the firm. Many media outlets will be only too grateful to know that, if a subject comes up on which you are qualified to speak, you will respond to an enquiry. In the context of time, be aware of the reality of the deadlines to which the media work, and do what can be done to accommodate them, but beware of being pressurised into making an over-hasty comment.

The issue of confidentiality

The knee-jerk reaction of many lawyers to any media enquiry (especially if client-related) is to offer a forceful 'no comment', pleading confiden-tiality. That may of course be both easy and appropriate, but some thought should be given to whether it actually best serves the interests of the client or the firm, as the case may be. It can undoubtedly, on occasion, be presented by the frustrated reporter as a deliberately and unjustifiably evasive response to what can be made to seem a simple question. If time permits, check as appropriate with the client (to whom any right of confidence belongs) or your partners as to whether a substantive response could be given without endangering the position, whether by allowing an interview or by giving a prepared statement. The latter will often appear more stilted, and hence be less effective, than an interview.

Coping with an interview

If being interviewed, there is no doubt that a lawyer needs to keep his wits about him. Bear in mind that the interviewer's aim is to produce a piece that is interesting to his audience, and that it is often the case that controversy produces interest. Be conscious also of the deadly effect of editing, so that one sentence, in an otherwise carefully reasoned statement, can be taken on its own. Try to avoid overlong responses, and avoid the temptation to speak simply to fill a pause – leave it to the interviewer to put the questions. Prepare for the interview insofar as you can. Make sure that you have the facts at your fingertips. Talk through with colleagues the sort of questions that might be asked, and work out what your approach to them should be. If you wish to adopt a politician's stance, and give your chosen comment as an answer, whatever the question, then be particularly well prepared (although any but old hands are best advised to avoid this tactic). If the interview is for television, then do give some thought to your personal appearance.

Networking

The other context in which any new partner is likely to find an increase in his public exposure is the myriad of networking opportunities. The professional world revolves largely around the making and developing of contacts, and any partner will be expected to play a part in this process. Some take to it like a duck to water, but some find the prospect of walking into a room full of comparative strangers to be daunting in the extreme. However, like most of the skills discussed in this chapter, it gets easier with practice! It may be helpful to prepare by considering in advance who is likely to be present and what you would like to discuss with them. It may be appropriate simply to take the opportunity to introduce yourself to people. On informal occasions, such as receptions and cocktail parties, others will expect this anyway. Even if they do not know you, they may well have heard of your firm, or know some of your partners, and may be interested to hear of your role in the organisation. Equally, remember that they are there to promote their firms just as much as you are, and are likely to welcome the chance for a new audience for their own firm's virtues. Properly used, informal networking is a key weapon in the armoury of a young partner seeking to make a name for himself. Make sure you have plenty of business cards to hand out, and that you in turn collect them from all those you have spoken to, if you feel you may wish to follow up the contact. Deal methodically with these cards, adding them to your contacts details once you are back at the office. Most important of all, if you have met someone about whom or whose business you wish to find out more, be pro-active in following up the first contact with a call, e-mail or letter within a relatively short period, when the initial contact is still fresh in the other party's mind.

Training possibilities

All of the matters canvassed in this section, i.e. making presentations, dealing with the media, and networking, are classic cases where some hands-on training may help enormously to build confidence. Acting out the various roles in a context where everyone else involved is also starting from the same position, and the only judgemental exercises will be of a practically helpful nature, is a great way to help someone to learn to relax into roles of this nature. Recording the session on video can help to show unconscious traits which it may be both desirable and simple to correct. A number of organisations offer suitable training. New partners may wish to suggest such training as an in-house exercise for their firms, so that several partners (and anyone else felt appropriate) can benefit on an economically acceptable basis. Quite simply, there is no substitute for trying out your skills.

Dealing with stress

The increase of stress in the workplace

One of the largest growth industries in recent times is that related to stress in the workplace. Supposedly, one of the most stressful environments in which to work is a law firm.[23] Stress has spilled over from the realms of human resources management into that of litigation, with a complex mix of employment law and personal injury law.[24] The term 'stress' is used to cover a whole spectrum of ailments, from an excuse used by an employee who really just fancies a couple of days off work, to the appalling harm that can follow a nervous breakdown and a consequent inability to work on what can be a very long-term basis. The difficulty that faces a manager is that he is very unlikely to be equipped to tell the difference between the two extremes. However, if he ignores the problem, and the need for it to be handled properly, in both substantive and procedural respects, he does so at his peril. Furthermore, a new partner should also be aware of warning signals of stress-related problems in his own life, as he adjusts to all the extra pressures of partnership.

Recognising the signs of stress

One of the most valuable functions a manager can undertake is to spot the signs of stress in a colleague, especially if that can be done before the colleague himself is willing to admit (perhaps even to himself) the extent of the problem. The sooner the matter can be addressed, the better the chances of overcoming the problem, and the greater the chance of nipping in the bud any consequent problems such as negligence or even fraud which may otherwise follow. Straightforward overwork is one endemic problem, but in a profession and a firm with a culture of long hours and intense client pressure, it may be difficult to distinguish from the normal levels of creative energy necessary for performance at a high level. Undoubtedly, however, work overload can be a major problem, and a partner with responsibilities for the allocation of work should keep that constantly in mind. Paradoxically, either persistent absenteeism or being present too much at the office, e.g. by not taking holidays, can both be symptomatic of stress. A reluctance to take time away from the office may indicate a knowledge that there are hidden problems which any holiday relief might discover. Excessive drinking, or taking drugs, may be linked to stress, although cause and effect may be difficult to distinguish. Abnormal behaviour patterns, e.g. sudden outbursts from someone who is normally equable, or withdrawal on the part of a normally gregarious colleague, can be indicators. So can certain physical illnesses which are commonly stress-related, such as stomach ulcers.

Managing stress

If he spots a stress problem, the first thing for a partner to realise is that he is unlikely to be able to deal with it on his own. Unless it is a very simple matter which can be addressed immediately, e.g. by reducing an individual's workload, then it is likely to be a team effort. If available, the HR manager, should be consulted, as the firm should have in place a policy for dealing with such matters. It is also likely that the person dealing with employment law matters within the firm should also be involved, as the way in which a problem is dealt with right from the moment of its recognition is vitally important. In addition to the employee's own doctor, it may be necessary to involve external agencies, such as any occupational physician who advises the firm, or a stress counsellor, or the legal profession's own dedicated resource, *LawCare*.[25] The individual's family may need to be considered. The team should act together in implementing a solution, working together with the affected individual, which firstly identifies the cause of the stress (which may not, of course, be work-related even if it is at work that the problem manifests itself) and then goes on to see what possible remedies can be identified.

Prevention of stress

Best practice is to ensure that stress is avoided in the first place. Firms should try to align their human resources policies in a way which will help in this respect. Many of the ideas canvassed in this chapter and in Chapter 6 will prove helpful by facilitating communication regarding problems and giving the flexibility to take corrective measures quickly. As mentioned, the firm should have a supportive policy, known to the staff, on how such problems will be approached. Some firms make stress counsellors freely available to staff. The costs of getting it wrong can be very high, in both personal terms as well as financial ones. The new partner should also bear in mind that partners may be the most vulnerable of all!

Information management skills

General

All new partners will, to a greater or lesser degree, already have been IT users before their promotion. Whether or not they are willing users is a different matter. There is still a great variety of attitudes towards IT, varying from those for whom it is an indispensable daily tool which they exploit to its fullest extent, to those who still regard it with suspicion. Perhaps curiously, there seems to be little hard evidence that this latter view is less prevalent in those coming more recently to the profession. It seems to be a function of the culture prevalent within the firms in which lawyers spend their early professional years, rather than a function of age itself. In most firms, however, any partner who wishes to be in a position to discharge his responsibilities as fully and easily as possible will almost certainly have to come to terms with direct involvement in the IT available to him. Practical familiarity with such basic programmes as Word®, Outlook® and Excel® should be supplemented by knowledge of any specific back office and case management software operated by the firm. Training and retraining facilities should be made available.

Additional IT facilities for partners

There may well be information, accessible only through use of the firm's IT facilities, which is confidential to partners, and to which staff such as secretaries will not therefore have access. Also this information may have been created using software with which junior staff may not be familiar, e.g. spreadsheets. Partners will have to consider making arrangements to familiarise themselves with necessary software. They may well need to utilise such facilities themselves, e.g. if called upon to present financial reports for their departments. Reference is made above to presentation software, and partners may need to learn how to use that as well. Any training will take time, and should also include time to practise using the software package.

Controlling management information

In addition to the above, partners must come to terms with the management of all the extra information which they have to handle as partners, i.e. over and above that received in their capacities as fee earners. Some of that task will be a question of understanding existing systems which are already established, e.g. personnel record systems. It may be necessary to sort out storage and retrieval systems for data created by others (e.g. the handling of monthly management accounting information, whether in electronic or paper format). There will also be a need for systematic treatment of any documents created by the partner, ranging from confidential partnership reports through to his own database of business contacts. The partner must, as early in his partnership career as possible, systematically determine the processes he wishes to use for these purposes.

Handling IT and data properly

A number of external matters will affect the parameters within which the firm's IT systems and the information held on them (and, indeed, in some cases, that held on paper-based record systems) can be operated. The first are legal requirements imposed on all businesses, led by the Data Protection Act 1998. Other legislative provisions include conflicting sets of regulations on e-mails, where the right to privacy vies with a firm's ability to know what is flowing through its communication media.[26] The firm should have a clear, understandable and internally well-publicised policy for all forms of data, internet and e-mail handling. If they have not, then any prudent new partner, for his own protection, should ensure that one is swiftly devised and promoted. The details of what should appear in these policies are beyond the scope of this work, and the reader should refer elsewhere[27] for more information, but the principle that both the firm's internal regulations and its legal obligations should be observed is clear.

Notes

1 Galanter, M. and Palay, T. (1991) *Tournament of Lawyers*, University of Chicago Press.
2 Handy, C. (1997) *The Hungry Spirit*, Hutchinson.
3 Radford, A. (1995) *Managing People in Professional Practices*, Institute of Personnel and Development, pp. 62 et seq quotes the instance of the programme at KPMG, where would-be partners are assessed on this and other personal qualities, as well as technical aspects, and are provided with a three-day development programme which includes time for reflection on personal goals.
4 Gold, J., Rodgers, H. and Smith, V. 'The Future of the Professions', (2001) Working Paper for the Council for Excellence in Management and Leadership, London.
5 On this particular point, partners should however remember that they are bound both legally and professionally, when considering partner admissions, not to discriminate.
6 Maister, D. (1993) *Managing the Professional Service Firm*, Free Press, Chapter 13.
7 Mayson, S. (1997) *Making Sense of Law Firms*, Blackstone Press, section 25.3.6.
8 Lorsch, J.W. and Tierney, J.T. (2002) *Aligning the Stars*, Harvard Business School Press.
9 Kaplan, R.S. and Norton, D.P (1996) *The Balanced Scorecard*, Harvard Business School Press.
10 Kaplan, R.S. and Norton, D.P (2001) *The Strategy-Focused Organization*, Harvard Business School Press, at pp. 244 et seq.
11 Moore, M. (2001) *Quality Management for Law Firms*, Law Society Publishing.
12 A failure to recognise and adapt to such limitations can lead to absurdity. The author recalls attending a conference where one speaker from the floor advocated the universal adoption of his personal solution, which was that he *never* accepted an incoming telephone call, but always instructed his secretary to arrange for him to place a return call within a pre-arranged time-frame. The fact that if this practice was taken up, it would mean that no-one would ever be able to speak to anyone, and that he was only able to maintain the practice by the tolerance of his fellow practitioners, had clearly escaped him!
13 Mayson, S. (1997) *Making Sense of Law Firms*, Blackstone Press, sections 3.6.1 and 28.4.
14 Such as Hooper, A. and Potter, J. (2000) *Intelligent Leadership – Creating a Passion for Change*, Random House.
15 Some academic institutions even have dedicated resources, such as the University of Exeter's Centre for Leadership Studies, featuring the authors named in the last note.
16 Maister, D. (2001) *Practice What You Preach*, Free Press, Chapter 7.
17 Ibid.
18 Rajan, A. and Van Eupen, P. (1997) *Leading People*, Create/Clintec.
19 Mayson, S. (1997) *Making Sense of Law Firms*, Blackstone Press, section 5.5.3.
20 Gold, J., Rodgers, H. and Smith, V. 'The Future of the Professions' (2001) Working Paper for the Council for Excellence in Management and Leadership, London.
21 Hammer, M. (1993) *Reengineering the Corporation*, Harper Collins.

22 Lambert, R. 'A Cycle of Change' (1993) Working Paper for Cranfield University School of Management.

23 Williams, S. (1999) *Report by Resource System for BUPA* (1998) *Law Society Gazette* 11 November, p.1.

24 See *Hatton* v. *Sutherland* [2002] 2 All ER 1.

25 Contactable via 0800279 6888, or **www.lawcare.org.uk**.

26 Telecommunications (Data Protection and Privacy) Regulations 1999, SI 1999/2093; the Telecommunications (Lawful Business Practice) (Interception of Communications) Regulations 2000, SI 2000/2699; and the Information Commissioner's 'Telecoms Guidance Note'.

27 Moore, M. (2001) *Quality Management for Law Firms*, Law Society Publishing, Chapter 14; Carey, P. and Ustaran, E. (2002) *E-privacy and On-line Data Protection*, Butterworths; Kendrick, R. (2000) *Managing Cyber-risks*, Law Society Publishing.

Further reading

Note that those books marked with an asterisk may be the most suitable for initial reading.

Adam, L. (2002) *Marketing Your Law Firm*, Law Society Publishing, London.

Allingham, S. and Mill, D. (2000) *Successful Law Firm Management,* W. Green & Son Ltd., Edinburgh.*

Belbin, R.M. (1981) *Management Teams: Why They Succeed Or Fail*, Butterworth-Heinemann, Oxford.

Belbin, R.M. (1993) *Team Roles At Work,* Butterworth-Heinemann, Oxford.

Bown-Wilson, D. and Courtney, G. (2002) *Marketing, Management and Motivation*, Law Society Publishing, London.

Grant, R. M. (1995) *Contemporary Strategy Analysis,* Blackwells, Oxford.

Hammer, M. (1996) *The Reengineering Revolution Handbook,* Harper Collins Publishers, London.

Handy, C. (1993) (4th edn) *Understanding Organizations,* Penguin Books, London.*

Hunt, J. W. (1992) (3rd edn) *Managing People At Work*, McGraw Hill, Maidenhead.

Kaplan, R. S. and Norton, D. P. (1996) *The Balanced Scorecard,* Harvard Business School Publishing, Boston.

Kaplan, R. S. and Norton, D. P. (2001) *The Strategy Focused Organisation,* Harvard Business School Publishing, Boston.

Lorsch, J. W. and Tierney, T. J. (2002) *Aligning the Stars,* Harvard Business School Publishing, Boston.

Maister, D. (1993) *Managing the Professional Service Firm*, The Free Press, New York.

Maister, D. (1997) *True Professionalism,* The Free Press, New York.

Maister, D. (2001) *Practice What You Preach,* The Free Press, New York.

Mayson, S. (1997) *Making Sense of Law Firms*, Blackstone Press, London.*

McDonald, M. and Payne, A. (1996) *Marketing Planning for Services*, Butterworth-Heinemann, Oxford.

Mintzberg, H. (1989) *Mintzberg on Management*, The Free Press, New York.

Moore, M. (2001) *Quality Management for Law Firms*, Law Society Publishing, London.*

Otterburn, A. (2002) *Profitability and Law Firm Management*, Law Society Publishing, London.*

Porter, M. E. (1980) *Competitive Strategy*, The Free Press, New York.

Porter, M. E. (1985) *Competitive Advantage*, The Free Press, New York.

Payne, A. (1993) *The Essence of Services Marketing*, Prentice Hall, Hemel Hempstead.

Radford, A. (1995) *Managing People in Professional Practices*, Institute of Personnel and Development, London.

Stewart, H. (2003) *Excellent Client Service*, Law Society Publishing, London.

Stutely, R. (1999) *The Definitive Business Plan*, Pearson Education Limited, London.*

Sources of Management Training

The following sources have been of assistance to the author and hence may be of interest to the reader.

BLS Professional Development, Denning House, 1 Hazelhurst Road, Worsley, Manchester, M28 2SX.

Central Law Training, Wrens Court, 52–54 Victoria Road, Sutton Coldfield, Birmingham B72 1SX.

Institute of Directors, 116 Pall Mall, London SW1Y 5ED.

Jordans Publishing, 21 St Thomas Street, Bristol, BS1 6JS.

Law Management Section, The Law Society, 113 Chancery Lane, London WC2A 1PL.

LawGroup (UK), Orbital House, 85 Croydon Road, Caterham, Surrey, CR3 6PD.

Nottingham Law School, Belgrave Centre, Chaucer Road, Nottingham, NG1 5LP.

Index